Nick Vandome

iPad

for Seniors

4th edition
covers all versions of iPad Mini and iPad 2 – iPad Air 2
with iOS 8

In easy steps is an imprint of In Easy Steps Limited
16 Hamilton Terrace · Holly Walk · Leamington Spa
Warwickshire · United Kingdom · CV32 4LY
www.ineasysteps.com

Fourth Edition

In Easy Steps Limited supports The Forest Stewardship Council (FSC),
the leading international forest certification organization. All our titles
that are printed on Greenpeace approved FSC certified paper carry the
FSC logo.

MIX
Paper from
responsible sources
FSC   FSC® C020837
www.fsc.org

Printed and bound in the United Kingdom

ISBN 978-1-84078-637-8

Contents

7 Staying Organized 113

8 Like a Good Book 129

9 Leisure Time 139

1 Choosing your iPad

It's compact, it's stylish, it's powerful, and it's perfect for anyone, of any age. This chapter introduces the iPad and its iOS 8 operating system so you can quickly get up and running with this exciting tablet.

Don't forget

'Apps' is just a fancy name for what are more traditionally called programs in the world of computing. The iPad has several apps that come built-in and ready for use. There are thousands more available for downloading from the online App Store (see Chapter Four, page 76).

Don't forget

The latest iPads, the iPad Air 2 and the iPad Mini 3, come with silver, space gray or gold back panels.

The New icon pictured above indicates a new or enhanced feature introduced with the latest version of iOS 8.

The iEverything

The iPad is a tablet computer that has gone a long way to change how we think of computers and how we interact with them. Instead of a large, static object it is effortlessly mobile and even makes a laptop seem bulky by comparison.

But even with its compact size, the iPad still manages to pack a lot of power and functionality into its diminutive body. In this case, small is very definitely beautiful and the range of what you can do with the iPad is considerable:

- Communicate via email, video and text messaging.

- Surf the Web wirelessly.

- Add an endless number of new 'apps' from the Apple App Store.

- Use a range of entertainment tools, covering music, photos, video, books and games.

- Do all of your favorite productivity tasks such as word processing, creating spreadsheets or producing presentations.

- Organize your life with apps for calendars, address books, notes, reminders and much more.

Add to this up to 10 hours' battery life when you are on the move, two different sizes (with a Retina Display screen of outstanding clarity) and a seamless backup system, and it is clear why the iPad can stylishly fulfil all of your computing needs.

Simplicity of the iPad

Computers have become a central part of our everyday lives, but there is no reason why they need to be complex devices that have us scratching our heads as to how to best use them. The iPad is not only stylish and compact, it also makes the computing process as simple as possible, so you can concentrate on what you want to do. Some ways in which this is done are:

- **Instantly on.** With the iPad there is no long wait for it to turn on, or wake from a state of sleep. When you turn it on, it is ready to use, it's as simple as that.

- **Apps.** iPad apps sit on the Home screen, visible and ready to use. Most apps are created in a similar format, so once you have mastered getting around them you will be comfortable using most apps.

- **Settings.** One of the built-in iPad apps is for Settings. This is a one-stop shop for customizing the way that your iPad looks and operates and also how settings for apps work.

- **Dock and Multitasking Window.** These are two functions that enable you to access your favorite apps quickly, regardless of what you are doing on your iPad.

- **Home button.** This enables you to return to the main Home screen at any time. It also has some additional functionality, depending on how many times you click it.

Hot tip

To set up the Touch ID functionality on an iPad Air 2 or an iPad Mini 3, access **Settings > Touch ID & Passcode** and drag the **Use Touch ID For** button to **On** for **iPad Unlock**. Tap once on the **Add a Fingerprint** button. You will be asked to create a passcode at this point, which is used if the Touch ID is unavailable. Then press your finger on the Home button until the Touch ID is created. This can then be used to unlock your iPad.

Don't forget

4G and 3G enables you to connect to a mobile network to access the Internet, in the same way as with a cell/mobile phone. This requires a contract with a provider of this type of service.

Models and Sizes

Since its introduction in 2010 the iPad has evolved in both its size and specifications. When choosing your iPad the first consideration is which size to select. There are two options:

- **Full size iPad.** This is the original size of the iPad. It measures 9.7 inches (diagonal) and has a high resolution Retina Display screen. The latest version, released in October 2014, is the iPad Air 2, which is the sixth generation of full size iPads.

- **iPad Mini.** The iPad Mini is similar in most respects to the larger version, including the Retina Display screen, except for its size. The screen is 7.9 inches (diagonal) and it is also slightly lighter. The latest version, also released in October 2014, is the iPad Mini 3.

The full size iPad Air 2 has a slightly faster processor than the iPad Mini 3. However, in terms of functionality there is little difference between the two and the choice may depend on the size of screen that you prefer and how portable you would like your iPad to be (the iPad Mini fits more easily into a smaller pocket or bag). Both the iPad Air 2 and the iPad Mini 3 have Touch ID functionality whereby the Home button can be used as a fingerprint sensor for unlocking the iPad with your unique fingerprint. Once this has been set up (see tip) your fingerprint can be used to unlock your iPad from the Lock Screen. It can also be used to authorize payment for items in the iTunes Store, iBooks and App Store (only in the US at the time of printing).

Another variation in the iPad family is how they connect to the Internet and online services. There are two options:

- **With Wi-Fi connectivity.** This enables you to connect to the Internet via a Wi-Fi router, either in your own home, or at a Wi-Fi hotspot.

- **With Wi-Fi and 4G connectivity (where available, but it also covers 3G).** This should be considered if you will need to connect to the Internet with a cellular connection when you are traveling away from home.

Specifications Explained

When choosing your iPad there are now a lot of available models, not just the most recent iPad Air 2 and iPad Mini 3. Some of the specifications to consider are:

- **Processor:** This determines the speed at which the iPad operates and how quickly tasks are performed.

- **Storage:** This determines how much content you can store on your iPad. Across the iPad family, the range of storage is 16GB, 32GB, 64GB or 128GB.

- **Connectivity:** The options for this are Wi-Fi and 3G/4G connectivity for the Internet, and Bluetooth for connecting to other devices over short distances.

- **Cameras.** The front-facing camera is a FaceTime one, which is best for video calls. The back-facing camera is a high resolution iSight one that takes excellent photos and videos.

- **Screen:** Look for an iPad with a Retina Display screen for the highest resolution and best clarity. This is an LED-backlit screen and is available on the latest iPads.

- **Operating System.** The full size version of the iPad and the iPad Mini both run on the iOS 8 operating system.

- **Battery power:** This is the length of time the iPad can be used for general use such as surfing the Web on Wi-Fi, watching video, or listening to music. All models offer approximately 10 hours of use in this way.

- **Input/Output:** These are a lightning connector port (for charging), 3.5 mm stereo headphone minijack, built-in speaker, microphone and nano-SIM card tray (Wi-Fi and 4G model only).

- **Sensors:** These are used to access the amount of ambient light and also the orientation in which the iPad is being held. The sensors include an accelerometer, ambient light sensor and gyroscope.

The amount of storage you need may change once you have bought your iPad. If possible, buy a version with as much as possible, as you cannot add more later.

The iSight camera on the iPad Air 2 is 8 megapixels and on other models it is 5 megapixels.

You can connect your iPad to a High Definition TV (HDTV), with AirPlay Mirroring. To do this you will need an Apple Lightning (or Dock) Digital AV Adapter or an Apple Lightning (or Dock) to VGA Adapter (sold separately).

To turn on the iPad, press and hold the **On/Off** button for a few seconds. It can also be used to Sleep the iPad or Wake it from the Sleep state.

The iPad Air 2 does not have a side switch, just two volume buttons.

If your iPad ever freezes, or if something is not working properly, it can be rebooted by holding down the Home button and the On/Off button for 10 seconds and then turning it on again by pressing and holding the Home button.

Before you Switch On

The external controls for the iPad are simple. Three of them are situated at the top of the iPad and the other is in the middle at the bottom. There are also two cameras, one on the front and one on the back of the iPad.

Controls

The controls at the top of the iPad are:

On/Off button

Side switch for silent mode (this applies to system sounds rather than the volume of items such as music or videos)

Volume Up or **Down** button

Cameras. One is located on the back, underneath the On/Off button and one on the front, top

Home button. Press this once to wake up the iPad or return to the Home screen at any point:

Speaker. The speakers are located on the bottom of the iPad:

Lightning connector. Connect the Lightning connector here to charge the iPad, or connect it to another computer. (See page 18 for more information on the connector for previous versions of the iPad.)

Getting Started

To start using the iPad, press the On/Off button once and hold it down for a few seconds.

Initially there will be a series of Setup screens to move through before you can use the iPad. These include the following options (a lot of these can be skipped during the Setup and accessed later from the **Settings** app):

- **Language.** Select the language you want to use.

- **Country.** Select the country in which you are located.

- **Location Services.** This determines whether your iPad can use your geographical location for apps that use this type of information (such as Maps).

- **Wi-Fi network.** Select a Wi-Fi network to connect to the Internet. If you are at home, this will be your own Wi-Fi network, if available. If you are at a Wi-Fi hotspot then this will appear on your network list.

- **Apple ID.** You can register with this to be able to access a range of Apple facilities, such as iCloud, purchase items on iTunes or the App Store, Facetime, Messages and iBooks. You can also create an Apple ID whenever you access one of the relevant apps for the first time.

- **iCloud.** This is Apple's online service for backing up content and sharing it with other people and family members, using the new Family Sharing service.

- **Find My iPad.** This is a service that can be activated so that you can locate your iPad if it is lost or stolen. This is done via the online iCloud site at **www.icloud.com**

- **Diagnostic information.** This enables information about your iPad to be sent to Apple.

- **Register.** This enables you to register your iPad with Apple, as the registered owner.

- **Start using.** Once the Setup process has been completed you can start using your iPad.

For details about obtaining an Apple ID see page 89.

For more information about using iCloud see pages 36-38.

The Find My iPad function can be set up within the **iCloud** sections of the **Settings** app (see pages 180-181).

iOS 8, the latest version of the operating system used by iPads, can be used on all iPads from the iPad 2 (second generation) onwards and all versions of the iPad Mini.

iOS 8 for the iPad does not contain the Health app; this is just on the iPhone.

To check the version of the iOS, look in **Settings > General > Software Update**.

About iOS 8

iOS 8 is the latest version of the operating system for Apple's mobile devices including the iPad, the iPhone and the iPod Touch.

iOS 8 is an evolution of iOS 7, which was one of the most dramatic cosmetic changes to the operating system in its history. It produced a flatter, cleaner, design and this has been continued with iOS 8, which is not greatly different in appearance to its predecessor.

Linking it all up

One of the features of iOS 8 is the way it links up with other Apple devices, whether it is something like an iPhone also using iOS 8, or an Apple desktop or laptop computer running the OS X Yosemite operating system. This works with apps such as Mail and Photos, so you can start an email on one device and finish it on another, or take a photo on one device and have it available on all other compatible Apple devices. Most of this is done through iCloud and once it is set up it takes care of most of these tasks automatically. (See pages 36-45 for details about setting up and using iCloud, Family Sharing and iCloud Drive.)

New and improved apps

Several of the iOS 8 apps have been updated and improved: the Messages app now enables group texts, video messages and displaying your locations; the Photos app has increased sharing capabilities; the Camera app now has a time lapse option; and the keyboard has an option for using predictive text. There is also a new Tips app and the iBooks and Podcasts apps are now built-in, saving the need to download them from the App Store.

iOS 8 is an operating system that is stylish and versatile on the iPad and it also plays an important role in the holy grail of computing: linking desktop and mobile devices so that users can spend more time doing the things that matter to them, safe in the knowledge that their content will be backed up and available across multiple devices.

Home Screen

Once you have completed the Setup process you will see the Home screen of the iPad. This contains the built-in apps:

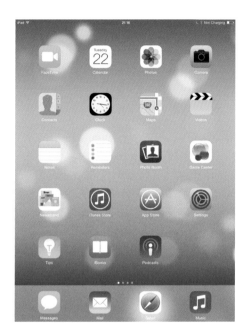

At the bottom of the screen are four apps that appear by default in the Dock area.

Rotate the iPad and the orientation changes automatically.

There are 39 different wallpaper backgrounds for iOS 8 on the iPad. These can be found in **Settings > Wallpapers.** Some of the wallpapers are **Dynamic**, which means that they appear to move independently from the apps icons when you tilt the iPad. The other backgrounds are **Stills** and you can also use your own pictures from the Photos app. The examples used in this book are from the dynamic range.

Items on the Dock can be removed and new ones can be added. For more details see pages 22-23.

Home Button

The Home button, located at the bottom, middle on the iPad, can be used to perform a number of tasks:

 Click once on the **Home** button to return to the Home screen at any point

 Double-click on the **Home** button to access the **Multitasking** window. This shows the most recently-used and open apps

Don't forget

The Multitasking window is also known as the App Switcher. See pages 24-25 for more details.

Don't forget

For more information about using the iPad search facilities, see pages 32-35.

Press and hold on the **Home** button to access the Siri voice assistant function

What can I help you with?

Opening Items

All apps on your iPad can be opened with the minimum of fuss and effort:

 Tap once on an icon to open the app

For details about closing items see page 25.

 The app opens at its Home screen

Click once on the **Home** button to return to the Home screen

 From the Multitasking window swipe between apps and tap on one to open it directly

Charging your iPad

The iPad comes with a Lightning connector to USB Cable and a USB Power Adapter, for charging the iPad:

 1 Connect the USB end of the Lightning connector to the Power Adapter

2 Connect the other end of the Lightning connector to the iPad

3 Plug in the Power Adapter

The iPad can also be charged by connecting it with the Lightning connector to another computer. However, this has to be another Mac computer and, if it is a MacBook, it also has to be plugged in for the iPad to charge.

2 Around your iPad

Once you have turned on your iPad you will want to start using it as soon as possible. This chapter shows how to do this, with details about settings, navigation, accessibility features and the voice assistant Siri. It also covers registering for and setting up the iCloud service for storing and backing up your content and also sharing it with other family members with Family Sharing.

iPad Settings

The Settings app is the one that should probably be explored first as it controls settings for the appearance of the iPad and the way it, and its apps, operate. To use the Settings app:

1 The Settings are listed down the left-hand side and the options are shown on the right-hand side

The System Settings are:

- **Airplane Mode.** This can be used while on an airplane.

- **Wi-Fi.** This enables you to select a wireless network.

- **Bluetooth.** Turn this On to connect Bluetooth devices.

- **Notifications.** This determines how the Notification Center operates (see pages 121-124).

- **Control Center.** This determines how the Control Center operates (see pages 26-27).

- **Do Not Disturb.** Use this to specify times when you do not want to receive audio alerts or FaceTime video calls.

- **General.** This contains a number of options for how the iPad operates. This is one of the most useful Settings.

- **Display & Brightness.** This can be used to set the screen brightness and text size and bold text.

- **Wallpaper.** This can be used to select a wallpaper.

- **Sounds.** This has options for setting sounds for alerts.

- **Passcode.** This has options for adding a passcode that is required whenever the Lock Screen is activated.

- **Privacy.** This can be used to activate Location Services so that your location can be used by specific apps.

- **iCloud.** This contains settings for items that are to be saved to the online iCloud.

- **iTunes & App Stores.** This can be used to specify downloading options for the iTunes and App Stores.

- **Mail, Contacts, Calendars.** This has options for how these three apps operate.

- **Notes.** This contains formatting options for creating items in the Notes app.

- **Reminders.** This has an option for syncing your reminders for other devices, covering a period of time.

- **Messages.** This can be used to sign in to the Messages app for sending and receiving text messages.

- **FaceTime.** This is used to turn video calling On or Off.

- **Maps.** This contains options for displaying distances and the default method for displaying directions.

- **Safari.** Settings for the Safari web browser.

- **Music.** This has options for how you listen to music.

- **Videos.** This has options for how you view videos.

- **Photos & Camera.** This has options for viewing and editing photos, slideshow settings and options for uploading to iCloud, and Photo Sharing options.

- **iBooks.** This contains options for reading books in the iBooks app, including hyphenation and using bookmarks.

- **Podcasts.** Use this for options for how podcasts are downloaded and synced to your iPad.

- **Game Center.** Use this set of options for playing games and inviting other players for multi-player games.

If you have an iPad with 3G/4G connectivity then there will also be a setting for Cellular.

Tap on a link to see additional options:

Tap once here to move back to the previous page for the selected Setting:

Using the Dock

By default, there are four apps on the Dock at the bottom of the screen. These are the four that Apple thinks you will use most frequently:

- **Messaging**, for text messages

- **Mail**, for email

- **Safari**, for web browsing

- **Music**

You can rearrange the order in which the Dock apps appear:

Hot tip

Just above the Dock is a line of small white dots. These indicate how many screens of content there are on the iPad. Tap on one of the dots to go to that screen.

 Tap and hold on one of the Dock apps until it starts to jiggle

 Drag the app into its new position

 Click once on the **Home** button to return from edit mode

Adding and removing Dock apps

You can also remove apps from the Dock and add new ones:

 To remove an app from the Dock, tap and hold it and drag it onto the main screen area

 To add an app to the Dock, tap and hold it and drag it onto the Dock

Don't forget

If items are removed from the Dock they are still available in the same way from the main screen.

The
number
of items
that can
be added
to the
Dock is
restricted
to a
maximum of six as the icons do not resize themselves

 Click once on the **Home** button to return from edit mode

Multitasking Window

The Multitasking feature in iOS 8 performs a number of shortcuts and useful tasks:

- It shows open apps

- It enables you to move between open apps and open different ones

- It enables apps to be closed (see next page)

Accessing Multitasking
The Multitasking option can be accessed from any screen on your iPad, as follows:

24

1 Double-click on the **Home** button

2 The currently-open apps are displayed, with their icons underneath them (except the Home screen). The most recently-used apps are shown first

3 Swipe left and right to view the open apps. Tap on one to access it in full screen size

Closing Items

The iPad deals with open apps very efficiently. They do not interact with other apps, which increases security and also means that they can be open in the background, without using up a significant amount of processing power, in a state of semi-hibernation until they are needed. Because of this it is not essential to close apps when you move to something else. However, you may want to close apps if you feel you have too many open or if one stops working. To do this:

1 Access the Multitasking window. The currently-open apps are displayed

2 Press and hold on an app and swipe it to the top of the screen to close it. This does not remove it from the iPad and it can be opened again in the usual way

3 The app is removed from its position in the Multitasking window

Don't forget

When you switch from one app to another, the first one stays open in the background. You can go back to it by accessing it from the Multitasking window or the Home screen.

Using the Control Center

The Control Center is a panel containing some of the most commonly used options within the **Settings** app. It can be accessed with one swipe and is an excellent function for when you do not want to have to go into Settings.

Accessing the Control Center

The Control Center can be accessed from any screen within iOS 8 and it can also be accessed from the Lock Screen:

 Tap once on the **Settings** app

 Tap once on the **Control Center** tab and drag the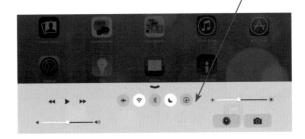
Access on Lock Screen and **Access Within Apps** buttons On or Off to specify if the Control Center can be accessed from there (if both are Off, it can still be accessed from any Home screen)

 Swipe up from the bottom of any screen to access the Control Center panel

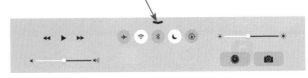

4 Tap on this button to hide the Control Center panel, or tap anywhere on the screen

Beware

The Control Center cannot be disabled from being accessed from the Home screen.

26

Control Center controls

The items that can be used in the Control Center are:

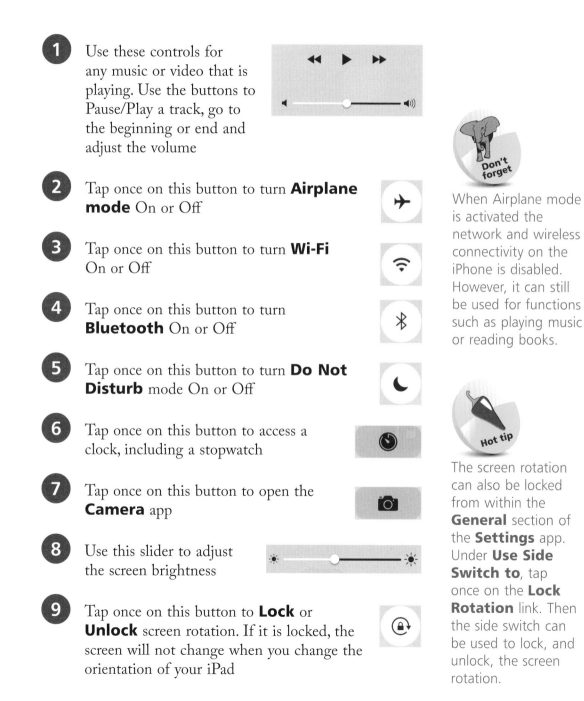

1 Use these controls for any music or video that is playing. Use the buttons to Pause/Play a track, go to the beginning or end and adjust the volume

2 Tap once on this button to turn **Airplane mode** On or Off

3 Tap once on this button to turn **Wi-Fi** On or Off

4 Tap once on this button to turn **Bluetooth** On or Off

5 Tap once on this button to turn **Do Not Disturb** mode On or Off

6 Tap once on this button to access a clock, including a stopwatch

7 Tap once on this button to open the **Camera** app

8 Use this slider to adjust the screen brightness

9 Tap once on this button to **Lock** or **Unlock** screen rotation. If it is locked, the screen will not change when you change the orientation of your iPad

Don't forget

When Airplane mode is activated the network and wireless connectivity on the iPhone is disabled. However, it can still be used for functions such as playing music or reading books.

Hot tip

The screen rotation can also be locked from within the **General** section of the **Settings** app. Under **Use Side Switch to**, tap once on the **Lock Rotation** link. Then the side switch can be used to lock, and unlock, the screen rotation.

Don't forget

Multitasking Gestures and Multitouch Gestures are the same and the terms are interchangeable.

Don't forget

You can also move between different screens by tapping once on the small white dots in the middle of the screen above the Dock.

Don't forget

You can also return to the Home screen by clicking once on the Home button.

Navigating Around

Most of the navigation on the iPad is done with Multitasking Gestures, which are looked at on the next three pages. Two of these can also be used for basic navigation:

Swiping between screens

Once you have added more apps to your iPad they will start to fill up more screens. To move between these:

Swipe left or right with one or two fingers.

Returning to the Home screen

Pinch together with thumb and four fingers to return to the Home screen from any open app.

Swipe, Tap and Pinch

Since there is no mouse connected to the iPad, navigation is done with your fingers. There is a combination of tapping, swiping and pinching gestures that can be used to view items such as web pages, photos, maps and documents and also navigate around the iPad.

Swiping up and down

Swipe up and down with one finger to move up or down web pages, photos, maps or documents. The content moves in the opposite direction of the swipe, i.e. if you swipe up, the page will move down and vice versa.

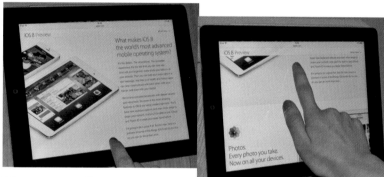

Hot tip

The faster you swipe on the screen, the faster the screen moves up or down.

Tapping and zooming

Double-tap with one finger to zoom in on a web page, photo, map or document. Double-tap with two fingers to return to the original view.

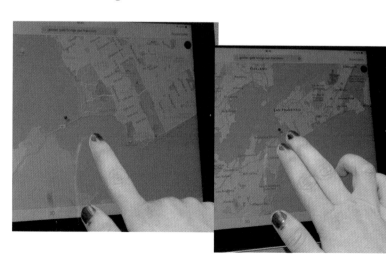

...cont'd

Pinching and swiping

Swipe outwards with thumb and forefinger to zoom in on a web page, photo, map or document.

Swiping outwards with thumb and forefinger enables you to zoom in on an item to a greater degree than double-tapping with one finger.

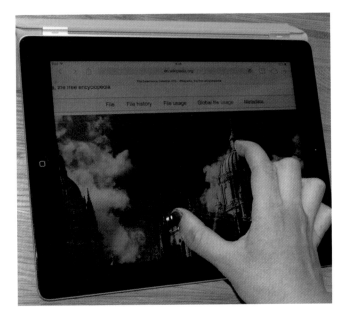

Pinch together with thumb and forefinger to zoom back out on a web page, photo, map or document.

More gestures

- Swipe left or right with four or five fingers to move between open apps

- Drag with two or three fingers to move a web page, photo, map or document

- Press and swipe down on any free area on the screen to access the Spotlight Search box

- Swipe left or right with one finger to move between full-size photos in the Photos app

- Tap once on a photo thumbnail with one finger to enlarge it to full screen within the Photos app

- Drag up from the bottom of the screen to access the Control Center

- Drag down at the top-middle of the iPad to view current notifications in the Notification Center

The Multitasking Gestures involving four or five fingers can be turned On or Off in the **General** section of the **Settings** app.

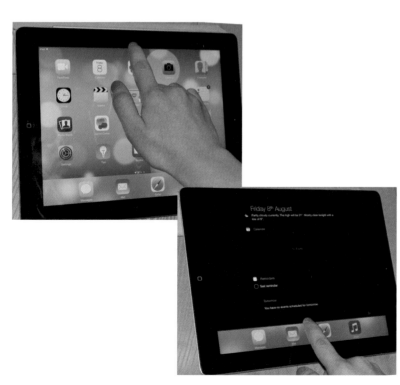

Finding Things with Siri

Siri is the iPad voice assistant that provides answers to a variety of questions by looking at your iPad and also web services. You can ask Siri questions relating to the apps on your iPad and also general questions, such as weather conditions around the world, or sports results. Initially, Siri can be set up within the **Settings** app:

 In the **General** section, tap once on the **Siri** link

 Drag the **Siri** button to **On** to activate the Siri functionality. Tap once on the links to select a language, set voice feedback and allow access to your details

Questioning Siri

Once you have set up Siri, you can start putting it to work with your queries. To do this:

 Hold down the **Home** button until the Siri window appears

 To find something from your iPad apps, ask a question such as, **Show me my reminders**

 Tap once on the microphone button to ask another question of Siri

Hot tip

Siri can be used to open any of the built-in iPad apps, simply by saying, **Open Photos**.

Siri can also find information from across the Web and related web services:

1 Siri can provide sports results, for certain sports in certain countries, such as in response to the question, **How did the Red Sox get on in their last match?**

The Red Sox were defeated by the Yankees on 28 September 2014; the final score was 9 to 5.

9-5
Final – 28 Sep 2014

	1	2	3	4	5	6	7	8	9	R	H	E
Yankees	0	0	4	0	0	0	5	0	0	9	12	1
Red Sox	0	0	0	0	0	0	5	0	0	5	5	0

Fenway Park – Boston

2 Weather reports are another of Siri's strong points and can even add in a bit of editorial comment in response to the question, **What is the weather like in Funchal, Portugal?**

Here's the forecast for Funchal, Portugal until 25 October 2014:

Funchal
Mostly Sunny

23°

Wednesday Today		23	17
Thursday		23	18
Friday		23	17
Saturday		23	17
Sunday		19	15
Monday		20	16
Tuesday		22	17
Wednesday		22	17

3 However, even Siri's knowledge is limited and if there is a subject it does not recognize it will provide details from Wikipedia or the Web instead

Here is what I found:

Wikipedia
Cricket

Cricket is a bat-and-ball game played between two teams of 11 players each on a field at the centre of which is a rectangular 22-yard long pitch. Each team takes its turn to bat, attempting to score runs, while the other team fields. Each turn is known as an innings. The bowler delivers the ball to the batsman who attempts to hit the ball with his bat away from the fielders so he can run to the other end of the pitch and score a run. Each batsman continues batting until he is out.

See full article

Don't forget

Siri can adapt to a number of different questioning styles, such as **Tell me about...**, **What is...**, **How can I get...**, and **How do I...**. The answers may be the same for each different style, although Siri may amend its comments, in the same way as people having a real conversation.

Searching with Spotlight

Siri can be used to search for items on your iPad and you can also use the built-in search engine, Spotlight. This can search over numerous items on your iPad and these can be selected within Settings:

Spotlight settings

Within the Settings app you can select which items the Spotlight search operates over. To do this:

Don't forget

To return to the Home screen from the Search page, tap once anywhere on the screen.

Hot tip

Enter the name of an app into the Spotlight search box and tap on the result to launch the app from here.

Don't forget

Spotlight can search over a range of areas, including nearby restaurants, movies and locations.

1 Tap once on the **Settings** app

2 Tap once on **General** tab

3 Tap once on the **Spotlight Search** link

Spotlight Search

4 Tap once on an item to exclude it from the Spotlight search. Items with a tick will be included

‹ General	Spotlight Search	
✓ Spotlight Suggestions		
✓ Contacts		
✓ Applications		
✓ Music		
Podcasts		
✓ Videos		
Audiobooks		

Accessing Spotlight

The Spotlight search box can be accessed from any Home screen by pressing and swiping downwards on any free area of the Home screen. This also activates the keyboard. Enter the search keywords into the search box at the top of the window

Picking Up Tips

Help is not far away with iOS 8 on your iPad, through the aid of the Tips app. This offers advice on using your iPad and the apps on it, such as Siri, Mail, Photos and also managing notifications. It comes preinstalled with iOS 8:

 Tap once on the **Tips** app

 Each tip has its own page.
Swipe left and right to move between the tips

 Tap once on this button to view the full table of contents for the Tips apps

35

The Tips app also has a Share button if you want to share a certain tip via Messages, Mail, Twitter or Facebook.

All Tips

Quickly respond to a notification

Notify me when there's a reply

Hey, Siri

Send a spoken message

Quickly manage your mail

Be in the shot

Come back soon

 The Tips app is updated on a regular basis so it is worth checking periodically to see if there is anything new

Living in the iCloud

iCloud is the Apple online service that performs a number of valuable functions:

It is free to register and set up a standard iCloud account.

- It makes your content available across multiple devices. The content is stored in the iCloud and then pushed out to other iCloud-enabled devices, including the iPhone, iPod Touch and other Mac or Windows computers.

- It enables online access to your content via the iCloud website. This includes your iCloud email, contacts, calendar and reminders.

- It backs up the content on your iPad.

Once you have registered for and set up iCloud, it works automatically so you do not have to worry about anything. You can activate iCloud when you first set up your iPad, or:

To access your iCloud account through the website, access www.icloud.com and enter your Apple ID details (see Chapter Five, page 89).

 Tap once on the **Settings** app

 Tap once on the **iCloud** tab

3 If you already have an Apple ID, enter your details here and tap once on **Sign In** button

| iCloud |
| nickvandome@mac.com |
| •••••••• |
| Sign In |
| Forgot Apple ID or Password? |
| Create a new Apple ID |

4 If you do not yet have an Apple ID, tap once on the **Create a new Apple ID** button and follow the steps to create your Apple ID

iCloud settings

Once you have set up your iCloud account you can then apply settings for how it works. Once you have done this you will not have to worry about it again:

 1 Access the **iCloud** section in the Settings app, as shown on the previous page

Once you have set up an iCloud account, your iCloud email appears on the iCloud button in Step 1.

2 Drag these buttons to On for each item that you wish to be included in iCloud. Each item is then saved and stored in the iCloud and made available to your other iCloud-enabled devices

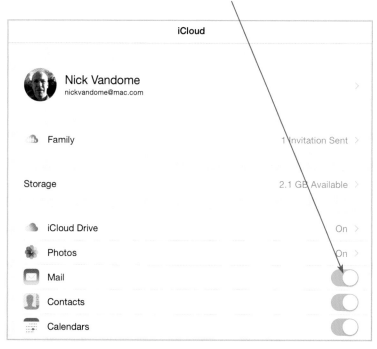

iCloud

Nick Vandome
nickvandome@mac.com

Family   1 Invitation Sent >

Storage   2.1 GB Available >

iCloud Drive   On >

Photos   On >

Mail

Contacts

Calendars

Tap once on the **Photos** button to access settings for storing and using your photos in iCloud. (See page 143 for more details about the settings for using photos with iCloud).

37

3 Tap once on the **iCloud Drive** button to see options for sharing your documents created with apps including Pages, Numbers and Keynote. See page 39 for more details about iCloud Drive

...cont'd

iCloud Storage & Backup

It is possible to view how the storage on your iCloud account is being used and also specify how your content is backed up to iCloud. To do this:

1 Access the iCloud section in the Settings app, as above, and tap once on **Storage**

Storage	2.5 GB Available >

2 Tap once on the **Manage Storage** link to view how your iCloud storage is being used

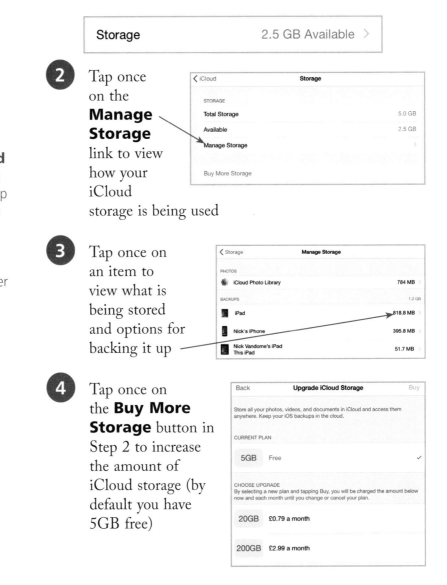

3 Tap once on an item to view what is being stored and options for backing it up

4 Tap once on the **Buy More Storage** button in Step 2 to increase the amount of iCloud storage (by default you have 5GB free)

About the iCloud Drive

One of the options in the iCloud section is for the Cloud Drive. This can be used to store documents so that you can use them on any other Apple devices that you have, such as an iPhone or a MacBook. With iCloud Drive you can start work on a document on one device and continue on another device from where you left off.

1 In the iCloud section of the Settings app, tap once on the **iCloud Drive** button

2 By default the iCloud Drive is set to **Off**

3 Tap once on the **iCloud Drive** button to turn it **On**

4 Drag the buttons **On** for the apps that you want to activate for sharing files with iCloud Drive. Content that you create with these apps will be stored in the iCloud Drive and be available with the same apps on other devices

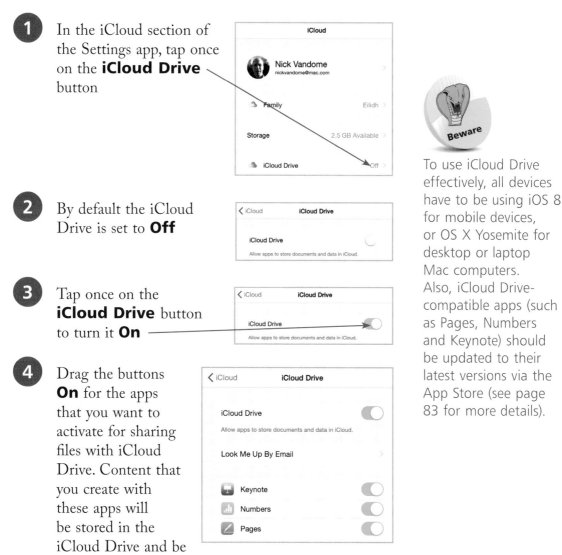

To use iCloud Drive effectively, all devices have to be using iOS 8 for mobile devices, or OS X Yosemite for desktop or laptop Mac computers. Also, iCloud Drive-compatible apps (such as Pages, Numbers and Keynote) should be updated to their latest versions via the App Store (see page 83 for more details).

About Family Sharing

As everyone gets more and more digital devices, it is becoming increasingly important to be able to share content with other people, particularly family members. In iOS 8 the Family Sharing function enables you to share items that you have downloaded from the App Store, such as music and movies, with up to six other family members, as long as they have an Apple Account. Once this has been set up it is also possible to share items such as family calendars, photos and even see where family members are within Maps. To set up and start using Family Sharing:

Don't forget

To use Family Sharing, other family members must have an Apple device using either iOS 8 for a mobile device (iPad, iPhone or iPod Touch) or OS X Yosemite for a desktop or laptop Mac computer.

1 Access the iCloud section within the Settings app, as shown on the previous pages

2 Tap once on the **Set Up Family Sharing** button

3 Tap once on the **Get Started** button

4 One person will be the organizer of Family Sharing, i.e. in charge of it, and if you set it up then it will be you. Tap once on the **Continue** button (the Family Sharing account will then be linked to your Apple ID)

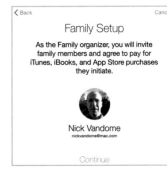

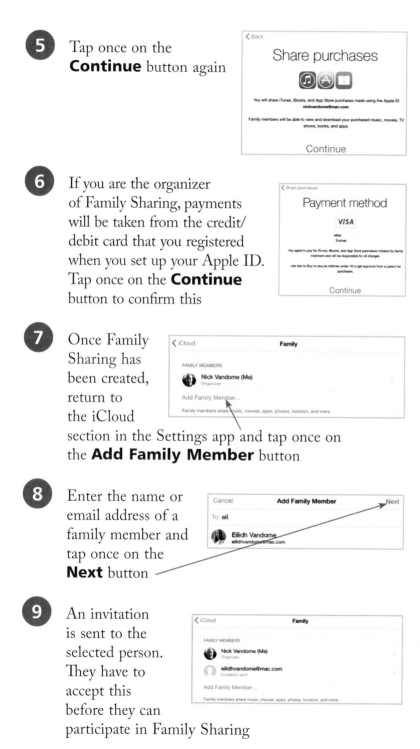

5 Tap once on the **Continue** button again

6 If you are the organizer of Family Sharing, payments will be taken from the credit/debit card that you registered when you set up your Apple ID. Tap once on the **Continue** button to confirm this

7 Once Family Sharing has been created, return to the iCloud section in the Settings app and tap once on the **Add Family Member** button

8 Enter the name or email address of a family member and tap once on the **Next** button

9 An invitation is sent to the selected person. They have to accept this before they can participate in Family Sharing

Hot tip

When you invite someone to Family Sharing you can specify that they have to ask permission before downloading content from the iTunes Store, the App Store or the iBooks store. To do this, select the family member in the **Family** section of the **iCloud** settings and drag the **Ask To Buy** button to **On**. Each time they want to buy something you will be sent a notification asking for approval. This is a good option if grandchildren are added to the Family Sharing group.

41

Using Family Sharing

Once you have set up Family Sharing and added family members you can start sharing a selection of items.

Sharing Photos

Photos can be shared with Family Sharing thanks to the Family album that is created automatically within the Photos app. To use this:

Beware

iCloud Photo Sharing has to be turned On to enable Family Sharing (**Settings > Photos & Camera > iCloud Photo Sharing**).

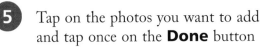

When someone else in your Family Sharing circle adds a photo to the Family album, you are notified in the Notification Center and also by a red notification on the Photos app.

1 Tap once on the **Photos** app

2 Tap once the **Shared** button

3 The **Family** album is already available in the **Shared** section. Tap once on the cloud button to access the album and start adding photos to it

4 Tap once on this button to add photos to the album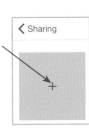

5 Tap on the photos you want to add and tap once on the **Done** button

6 Make sure the **Family** album is selected as the Shared Album and tap once on the **Post** button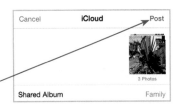

Sharing Calendars

Family Sharing also generates a Family calendar that can be used by all Family Sharing members:

1 Tap once on the **Calendar** app

2 Tap once the **Calendars** button to view the Family calendar

✓ • Family
Shared with Eilidh Vandome (i)

OTHER

✓ • UK Holidays
Subscribed (i)

Calendars

3 Press and hold on a date to create a New

Calendar   • Home >

Event. The current calendar will probably not be the Family one. Tap once on the calendar to change it

4 Tap once on the **Family** calendar

• Work

• Birthdays

Family ✓
Shared with Eilidh Vandome

5 The **Family** calendar is now the active one

Calendar   • Family >

6 Complete the details for the event. It will be added to your calendar, with the Family color tag. Other people in your Family Sharing circle

18   19
Family BBQ   Brown

25   26
Summer bank holiday...

will have this event added to their Family calendar too and they will be sent a notification

44

Don't forget

For more details about using the App Store, see pages 76-81.

Don't forget

Tap once on the **Add** button to invite other people by email (they do not have to be part of Family Sharing, but they do have to accept your invitation to be part of Find My Friends).

Add

Don't forget

Tap once on your own name at the bottom-left of the screen to see your settings for Find My Friends.

Me
Great Britain

...cont'd

Finding family members

Family Sharing makes it easy to keep in touch with the rest of the family and see exactly where they are. This can be done with the Find My Friends app. The other person must have their iPad (or other Apple device) turned on and online. To find family members:

1 Tap once on the **App Store** app

App Store

2 Type **find my friends** into the Search box

3 Tap once on the **Free** button next to the Find My Friends app

4 Tap once on the **Open** button

5 The location of any people who are linked via your Family Sharing is displayed. Tap once on a person's name to view their location. Swipe outwards with thumb and forefinger to zoom in on the map

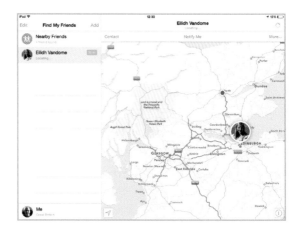

Sharing music, books and movies

Family Sharing means that all members of the group can share purchases from the iTunes Store, the App Store or the iBooks store. To do this:

1 Open either **iTunes Store**, **App Store** or **iBooks**

2 Tap once on the **Purchased** button

3 Tap once on the **My Purchases** button in the top left-hand corner

4 Tap once on a member under **Family Purchases** to view their purchases

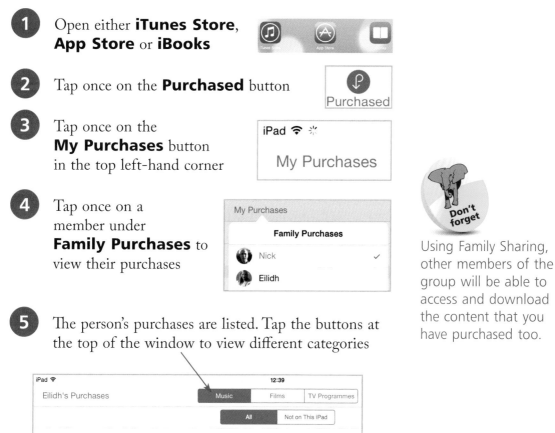

5 The person's purchases are listed. Tap the buttons at the top of the window to view different categories

6 Tap once on this button next to an item to download it to your iPad

Using Family Sharing, other members of the group will be able to access and download the content that you have purchased too.

Don't forget

If your iOS software is up-to-date there is a message to this effect in the **Software Update** window.

Hot tip

It is always worth updating the iOS to keep up-to-date with fixes. Also, app developers update their products to use the latest iOS features.

Updating Software

The operating system that powers the iPad is known as iOS. This is a mobile computing operating system and it is also used on the iPhone and the iPod Touch. The latest version is iOS 8. Periodically, there are updates to the iOS to fix bugs and add new features. These can be downloaded to your iPad once they are released:

 Tap once on the **Settings** app

 Tap once on the **General** tab

 Tap once on the **Software Update** link

Software Update 　　　　　　　　　　　　　　　　　　＞

④ If there is an update available it will be displayed here, with details of what is contained within it

 Tap once on the **Download and Install** button to start the downloading process. The iOS update will then be done automatically

Using the Lock Screen

To save power it is possible to set your iPad screen to auto-lock. This is the equivalent of the sleep option on a traditional computer. To do this:

1 Tap once on the **Settings** app

2 Tap once on the **General** tab

3 Tap once on the **Auto-Lock** link

Auto-Lock	Never >

4 Tap once on the time of non-use after which you wish the screen to be locked

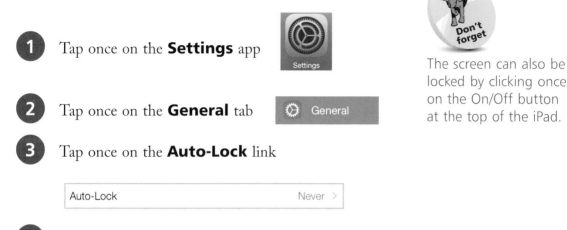

5 Once the screen is locked, swipe here to the right to unlock the screen

The screen can also be locked by clicking once on the On/Off button at the top of the iPad.

Auto-locking the screen does not prevent other people from accessing your iPad. If you want to prevent anyone else having access, it can be locked with a passcode. See page 182 for details.

iPad Smart Cover

To prevent the iPad screen getting scratched, a cover (known as a Smart Cover) can be used as protection. This can also be used as a stand to support the iPad for viewing content or typing with the keyboard.

There are settings for the iPad cover in the Settings app. This can enable it to lock or unlock the iPad:

Smart Covers are made from polyurethane and come in several different colors. There are also Smart Cases which are made from leather and cover the front and back of the iPad and come in five different colors.

1 Tap once on the **Settings** app

2 Tap once on the **General** tab

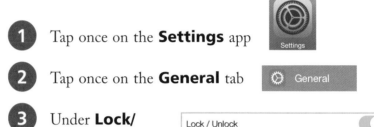

3 Under **Lock/ Unlock** drag the button to **On** to enable the cover to lock or unlock the iPad when it is placed in position or removed

Attaching the cover
The iPad cover attaches with a hinge along the left-hand side of the iPad. Attach it by placing the hinge on the side of the iPad until it clicks magnetically into place.

Use the stand at the top of the iPad when using the keyboard for input options. Use it at the bottom of the iPad when viewing content such as videos or photos.

Using the cover as a stand
The iPad cover is separated into four foldable panels. These can be folded into a triangular shape to create a stand for the iPad.

Accessibility Issues

The iPad tries to cater to as wide a range of users as possible, including those who have difficulty with vision, hearing or physical and motor issues. There are a number of settings that can help with these areas. To access the range of accessibility settings:

 Tap once on the **Settings** app

 Tap once on the **General** tab

⚙ General

 Tap once on the **Accessibility** link

Accessibility	>

4 The settings for **Vision**, **Hearing**, **Learning** and **Physical & Motor** are displayed here

‹ General	Accessibility	
VISION		
VoiceOver	Off	>
Zoom	Off	>
Invert Colors		◯
Grayscale		◯
Speech		>
Larger Text	Off	>
Bold Text		◯
Button Shapes		◯

You may have to scroll down the page to view and access the Accessibility link.

VoiceOver works with the built-in iPad apps and some apps from the App Store, but not all of them.

...cont'd

Vision settings

These can help anyone with impaired vision and there are options to hear items on the screen and also for making text easier to read:

When VoiceOver is On, tap once on an item to select it and have it spoken; double-tap to activate the item.

1 Tap once on the **VoiceOver** link

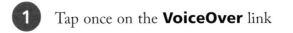

VoiceOver	Off >

2 Drag this button to **On** to activate the VoiceOver function. This then enables items to be spoken when you tap on them

❮ Accessibility **VoiceOver**

VoiceOver

VoiceOver speaks items on the screen:
· Tap once to select an item
· Double-Tap to activate the selected item
· Swipe three fingers to scroll

VoiceOver Practice

50

There is a wide range of options for the way VoiceOver can be used. For full details see the Apple website at **www.apple.com/ accessibility/ios/**

3 Select options for VoiceOver as required

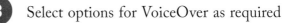

SPEAKING RATE

Speak Hints

Use Pitch Change

Use Sound Effects

...cont'd

4 Tap once on the **Accessibility** button to return to the main options

⟨ Accessibility

5 Tap once on these buttons to access options for zooming the screen, increasing text size, changing the text color on the screen and speaking text

VISION

VoiceOver	Off >
Zoom	Off >
Invert Colors	◯
Grayscale	◯
Speech	>

6 Tap once on the **Accessibility** button to return to the main options after each selection

Hearing settings

These can be used to change the iPad speaker from stereo to mono. To do this:

1 Drag this button to On to enable **Mono Audio**

HEARING

| Subtitles & Captioning | > |
| Mono Audio | ◯ |

L ———————————◯——————————— R

Adjust the audio volume balance between left and right channels.

2 Drag this button to specify whether sound comes out of the left or the right side of the speaker

Don't forget

If you turn on the **Zoom** function you can magnify the whole screen by double-tapping twice. To move around the screen, drag with three fingers. To change the amount of zoom, double-tap with three fingers and drag up or down on the screen.

51

Hot tip

The **Speak Auto-text** function can be turned on so that auto-corrections and auto-capitalizations are automatically spoken.

...cont'd

AssistiveTouch

This can be used by anyone who has difficulty navigating around the iPad with the screen or buttons. It can be used with an external device such as a joystick, or it can be used on its own. To use AssistiveTouch:

 Tap once on the **AssistiveTouch** link

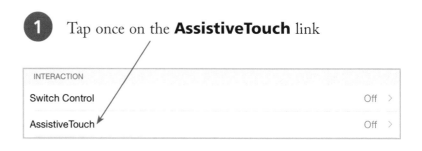

INTERACTION

Switch Control   Off >

AssistiveTouch   Off >

52

The **AssistiveTouch** options make it easier for anyone with difficulties clicking the Home button, or using Multitasking Gestures.

2 Drag this button to **On** to activate the **AssistiveTouch** function

‹ Accessibility   **AssistiveTouch**   Edit

AssistiveTouch   ⬭

3 The AssistiveTouch icon appears on the screen and can be dragged around

4 Tap once on the AssistiveTouch icon to view its options

5 Tap once on the **Home** icon to return to the Home screen

6 Tap once on the **Favorites** icon to access options for using custom gestures

Favorites

7 To create a custom gesture, tap once on this link under the AssistiveTouch section

Create New Gesture... >

Don't forget

The **Gestures** section can be used to perform Multitasking Gestures, without having to physically use the full number of fingers on the screen.

8 Drag on the screen with the required gesture (e.g. swiping with four fingers to move between open apps)

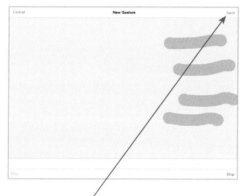

9 Tap once on the **Save** button

10 Give the gesture a name and tap once on the **Save** button

New Gesture

Swipe apps

Cancel | Save

Hot tip

The **Favorites** section can also be used to create custom gestures. To do this, tap once on one of the empty boxes and then record the gesture in the **New Gesture** window. Once it is saved it becomes available in the Favorites section.

11 The gesture is added under the Favorites section

12 Tap once on a gesture to select it. The corresponding number of blue circles appear. Tap on one to activate the gesture

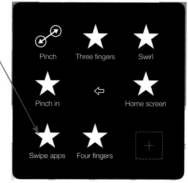

Pinch · Three fingers · Swirl
Pinch in · Home screen
Swipe apps · Four fingers

...cont'd

 Tap once on the **Device** icon

Tap on the **More** button in the **Device** window to select options for creating more gestures, shaking the iPad, capturing a screenshot and accessing the Multitasking window.

54

 Tap once to activate the required function, including changing the screen rotation and adjusting the volume

Guided Access

The Guided Access option allows for certain functionality within an app to be disabled so that individual tasks can be focused on without any other distractions. To use this:

 Under the Learning heading tap once on the **Guided Access** link

LEARNING

Guided Access   Off >

When you first activate Guided Access for an app you will need to enter a passcode. This must also be entered when you leave Guided Access.

 Drag this button to **On** to activate the Guided Access functionality

< Accessibility   **Guided Access**

Guided Access

Guided Access keeps the iPad in a single app, and allows you to control which features are available. To start Guided Access, Triple-Click the Home button in the app you want to use.

Passcode Settings

Time Limits

Accessibility Shortcut

When you Triple-Click the Home button while Guided Access is enabled, your Accessibility Shortcut settings will be displayed.

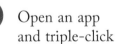 Open an app and triple-click on the **Home** button to activate Guided Access within the app

 Circle an area on the screen to disable it (this can be any functionality within the app). Tap on the **Start** button to activate Guided Access for that app. The circled area will not function within the app

3 The iPad Keyboard

The iPad has a virtual keyboard rather than a traditional one. This chapter shows how to use it for entering standard or predictive text and also editing text and adding shortcuts.

It's Virtually a Keyboard

The keyboard on the iPad is a virtual one, i.e. it appears on the touch screen whenever text or numbered input is required for an app. This can be for a variety of reasons:

- Entering text with a word processing app, email or an organizing app such as Notes

- Entering a web address in a web browser such as the Safari app

- Entering information into a form

- Entering a password

Viewing the keyboard

When you attempt one of the items above, the keyboard appears so that you can enter any text or numbers:

Around the keyboard

To access the various keyboard controls:

In addition to the iPad virtual keyboard, it is also possible to use a traditional computer keyboard with the iPad. This can be particularly useful if you are using the iPad for a lot of typing. The keyboard is an Apple Wireless Keyboard which connects via Bluetooth. This can be turned on in the Settings app, under the Bluetooth tab.

1 Tap once on the Shift button to create a **Cap** (capital) text letter

2 Double-tap on the Shift button to create **Caps Lock**

To return from Caps Lock, tap once on the Caps button.

3 Tap once on this button to back delete an item

56

4 Tap once on this button to access the **Numbers** keyboard option

.?123

| 1 | 2 | 3 | 4 | 5 | 6 | 7 | 8 | 9 | 0 | ⌫ |

| - | / | : | ; | (|) | £ | & | @ | return |

| #+= | undo | . | , | ? | ! | ' | " | #+= |

| ABC | 🌐 | 🎤 | | ABC | ⌨ |

Hot tip

If you are entering a password, or details into a form, the keyboard will have a **Go** or **Send** button that can be used to activate the information that has been entered.

5 From the Numbers keyboard, tap once on this button to access the **Symbols** keyboard

#+=

| [|] | { | } | # | % | ^ | * | + | = | ⌫ |

| _ | \ | | | ~ | < | > | € | $ | ¥ | return |

| 123 | redo | . | , | ? | ! | ' | " | 123 |

| ABC | 🌐 | 🎤 | | ABC | ⌨ |

57

6 Tap once on this button on either of the two keyboards above to return to the standard QWERTY option

ABC

Hot tip

The button in Step 7 can also be used to undock and move the keyboard. For details see pages 64-65.

7 Tap once on this button to hide the keyboard (this can be done from any of the keyboard options). If the keyboard is hidden, tap once on one of the input options, e.g. entering text, to show it again

Keyboard Settings

Settings for the keyboard can be determined in the General section of the Settings app. To do this:

1 Tap once on the **Settings** app

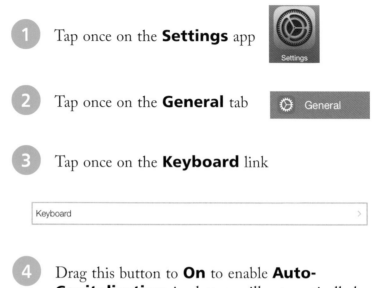

2 Tap once on the **General** tab

3 Tap once on the **Keyboard** link

Keyboard	>

4 Drag this button to **On** to enable **Auto-Capitalization**, i.e. letters will automatically be capitalized at the beginning of a sentence

Auto-Capitalization	◯

5 Drag this button to **On** to enable **Auto-Correction**, i.e. suggestions for words will appear as you type, particularly if you have mis-typed a word

Auto-Correction	◯

6 Drag this button to **On** to check spelling as you type

Check Spelling	◯

Hot tip

The Auto-Correction function works as you type a word, so it may change a number of times, depending on the length of the word you are typing.

58

7 Drag this button to **On** to enable the **Caps Lock** function to be performed

Enable Caps Lock

8 Drag this button to **On** to enable the **Shortcut** functionality

"." Shortcut

For more information about keyboard shortcuts, see pages 66-67.

9 Drag this button to **On** to enable the keyboard to be split and moved. Tap once on the Keyboards link to access options for adding different international keyboards

Keyboards   1 >

Split Keyboard

10 Tap once on this link to view existing text shortcuts and also to create new ones

SHORTCUTS

omw   On my way >

Add New Shortcut...

11 Tap once on this link to create new shortcuts

Entering Text

Once you have applied the keyboard settings that you require you can start entering text. To do this:

1 Tap once on the screen to activate the keyboard. Start typing with the keyboard. The text will appear at the point where you tapped on the screen

Don't forget

If you keep typing as normal, the Auto-Correction suggestion will disappear when you finish the word.

2 As you type, Auto-Correction comes up with suggestions. Tap once on the spacebar to accept the suggestion, or tap once on the cross next to it to reject it

3 If Check Spelling is enabled, any misspelled words appear underlined in red

Remember to go to the supermrket |

4 Tap once on this button to hide the keyboard

Editing Text

Once text has been entered it can be selected, copied, cut and pasted. Depending on the app being used, the text can also be formatted, such as with a word processing app.

Selecting text

To select text and perform tasks on it:

1 To change the insertion point, tap and hold until the magnifying glass appears

Hot tip

Once the selection buttons have been accessed, tap once on **Select** to select the previous word, or **Select All** to select all of the text.

2 Drag the magnifying glass to move the insertion point

Hot tip

The selection buttons in Step 4 can also be used to replace the selected word, add bold, italics or underlining to it, or view a definition of it.

3 Tap once at the insertion point to access the selection buttons

4 Double-tap on a word to select it. Tap once on **Cut** or **Copy** as required

5 Drag the selection handles to expand or contract the selection

Don't forget

Some apps that allow text entry have formatting options, while others do not and text is just entered in a standard format.

6 If text has been copied, tap and hold at a new point on the page and tap once on **Paste**

Using Predictive Text

Predictive text tries to guess what you are typing and also predict the next word following the one you have just typed. It was developed primarily for text messaging and it has now been introduced to the iPad with iOS 8. To use it:

 Tap once on the **General** tab in the Settings app

 Tap once on the **Keyboard** link

Keyboard	⟩

③ Drag the **Predictive** button **On**

④ When predictive text is activated the QuickType bar is displayed above the keyboard. Initially this has a suggestion for the first word to include. Tap on a word or start typing

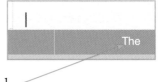

Predictive text learns from your writing style as you write and so gets more accurate at predicting words.

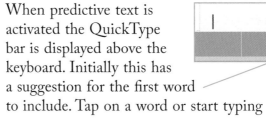

5 As you type, suggestions appear. Tap on one to accept it. Tap on the word within the quotation marks to accept exactly what you have typed

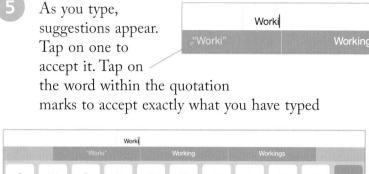

6 After you have typed a word a suggestion for the next word appears. This can be used by tapping on it, or ignored

Toggling predictive text from the keyboard

You can also toggle predictive text On or Off from the keyboard. To do this:

1 Press on this button on the keyboard

2 Drag the **Predictive** button to turn it **On** or **Off**

Moving the Keyboard

By default, the keyboard appears as a single unit along the bottom of the screen. However, it is possible to split the keyboard so that it appears on separate sides of the screen. It is also possible to undock the keyboard and move it around the screen.

Undocking the keyboard

To undock the keyboard from its position at the bottom of the screen:

Hot tip

To redock the keyboard, tap and hold on the button in Step 1 and tap once on the **Dock** button.

 Press and hold on this button on the keyboard

 Tap once on the **Undock** button

 The keyboard is undocked from the bottom of the screen

 Press and drag on the keyboard button to move the keyboard

The keyboard can then be moved to different positions around the screen

...cont'd

Splitting the keyboard

The keyboard can also be split into two and used on either side of the screen. To do this:

1 Press and hold on this button on the keyboard

2 Tap once on the **Split** button

Beware

When the keyboard is split, both sides can be a bit small and it is a bit more fiddly than using the full-size keyboard.

3 The keyboard is split to the left and the right sides of the screen

65

4 Press and drag here to move the split keyboard

Hot tip

The keyboard can also be split by swiping outwards on both sides, with one finger on each side. Reverse the process to merge it again.

5 Press and hold on the button above and tap once on the **Dock and Merge** button to return the keyboard to its default position at the bottom of the screen

Keyboard Shortcuts

There are two types of shortcuts that can be used on the iPad keyboard:

- Shortcuts on the keys on the keyboard

- Shortcuts created with text abbreviations

Shortcuts with keys

The shortcuts that can be created with the keys on the keyboard are:

1 Double-tap on the spacebar to add a full stop/period and a space at the end of a sentence

2 Swipe up once on the comma (or press and hold) to insert an apostrophe

3 Swipe up once on the full stop/period to insert quotation marks

4 Press and hold on appropriate letters to access accented versions for different languages

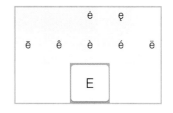

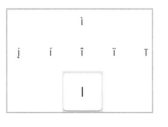

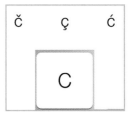

Text abbreviations

To create shortcuts with text abbreviations:

1 Tap once on the **Keyboard** link in the **General** section of the Settings app

Keyboard	⟩

2 Tap once on the **Shortcuts** link

Shortcuts	⟩

3 Tap once on this button to add a new shortcut ➕

4 Enter the phrase you want to be made into a shortcut

Phrase	My name is Nick

5 Enter the abbreviation you want to use as the shortcut for the phrase

Shortcut	mnn

6 Tap once on the **Save** button

Save

7 The shortcut is displayed here

‹ Keyboards	**Shortcuts**	+
Q Search		A B C
M		
mnn	My name is Nick	D E
O		F
omw	On my way	G

8 Use the Search box or the alphabetical bar at the right-hand side to search for other shortcuts that have been created

Beware

An abbreviation for a shortcut must have a minimum of two characters.

Don't forget

The shortcut does not need to have the equivalent number of letters as words in the phrase. A 10-word phrase could have a two-letter shortcut.

Hot tip

To use a shortcut, enter the abbreviation. As you type, the phrase appears underneath the abbreviation. Tap once on the spacebar to add the phrase, or tap once on the cross to reject it. To delete a shortcut, swipe on it from right to left and tap once on the **Delete** button.

Adding Third-Party Keyboards

In iOS 8 it is now possible to use other keyboards with the iPad, other than the default one that is provided. There are some keyboard apps available in the App Store and this number is likely to grow as more developers create their own keyboards, with new features and options. A lot of these keyboards allow users to enter text by swiping over the keys on the keyboard. To use a third-party keyboard:

Don't forget

For more details about using the App Store and finding apps, see pages 76-82.

Hot tip

Some third-party keyboards to look at include SwiftKey, Swype and KuaiBoard.

Beware

If you just type 'keyboard' into the App Store search box you will probably get a lot of musical keyboard suggestions.

68

1 Tap once on this button to open the App Store

2 Type the name of a keyboard into the search box and tap once on one of the options

3 Tap once on the app's price or **Free** button and tap once on the **Install** button

4 Tap once on the **Open** button or tap on the app's icon on the Home screen

Using a new keyboard

Once you have downloaded a new, third-party keyboard you have to add it within the Settings app. To do this:

1 Tap once on the **Settings** app

2 Tap once on the **General** tab

⚙ General

3 Tap once on the **Keyboard** button

| Keyboard | > |

4 Tap once on the **Keyboards** button

❮ General   **Keyboards**

Keyboards   2 >

5 Tap once on the **Add New Keyboard** button

Add New Keyboard...   >

6 Tap once on the keyboard you want to add

Cancel   **Add New Keyboard**

SUGGESTED KEYBOARDS

English (UK)

THIRD-PARTY KEYBOARDS
When using one of these keyboards, the keyboard can access all the data you type.
About Third-Party Keyboards & Privacy...

SwiftKey

Hot tip

The process on this page can also be used for adding different language keyboards.

7 The keyboard is added to the **Keyboards** list within the Settings app

❮ Keyboards   **Keyboards**   Edit

English (UK)   >

Emoji

SwiftKey — SwiftKey
Multiple Languages   >

8 Open the default keyboard and tap on this button until the required one appears

🌐

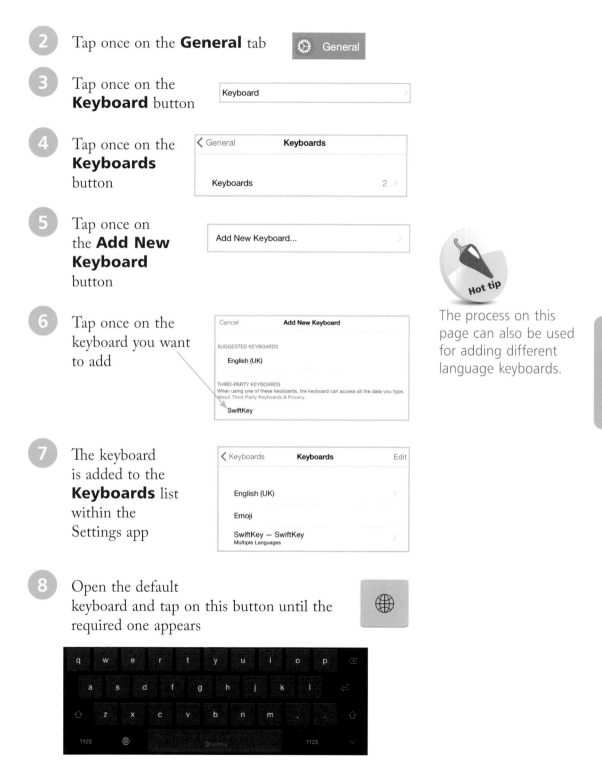

Voice Typing

On the keyboard there is also a voice typing option, which enables you to enter text by speaking into a microphone, rather than typing on the keyboard. This is On by default.

Using voice typing

Voice typing can be used with any app with a text input function. To do this:

Beware

Voice typing is not an exact science and you may find that some strange examples appear. The best results are created if you speak as clearly as possible and reasonably slowly.

1 Tap once on this button on the keyboard to activate the voice typing microphone. Speak into the microphone to record text

2 As the voice typing function is processing the recording this screen appears

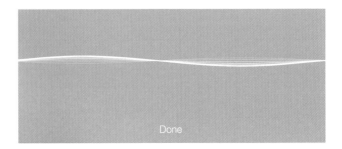

Done

3 Tap once on the **Done** button to finish recording

4 Once the recording has been processed the text appears in the app

Don't forget

There are other voice typing apps available from the App Store. Two to try are Dragon Dictation and Voice Dictation.

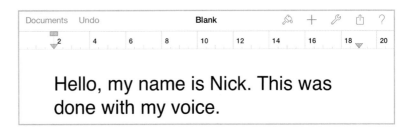

Documents Undo   **Blank**

2   4   6   8   10   12   14   16   18   20

Hello, my name is Nick. This was done with my voice.

4 Knowing your Apps

Apps keep the iPad engine running. This chapter details the built-in ones and shows how to obtain more through the App Store.

What is an App?

An app is just a more modern name for a computer program. Initially, it was used in relation to mobile devices, such as the iPhone and the iPad, but it is now becoming more widely used with desktop and laptop computers, for both Mac and Windows operating systems.

On the iPad there are two types of apps:

Don't forget

You need an active Internet connection to download apps from the App Store.

- **Built-in apps.** These are the apps that come pre-installed on the iPad.

- **App Store apps.** These are apps that can be downloaded from the online App Store. There is a huge range of apps available there, covering a variety of different categories. Some are free while others have to be paid for. The apps in the App Store are updated and added to on a daily basis so there are always new ones to explore.

There are also two important points about apps (both built-in and those from the App Store) to remember:

Hot tip

Within a number of apps there is a **Share** button that can be used to share items through a variety of methods, including email, Facebook and Twitter. For the iPad 4 and later and the iPad Mini, the Share button can also be used to share items using the AirDrop function over short distances with other compatible devices. To access these options, tap once on this button, where available.

- Apart from some of the built-in apps, the majority of apps do not interact with each other. This means that there is less chance of viruses being transmitted from app to app on your iPad and they can operate without a reliance on other apps.

- Content created by apps is saved within the app itself, rather than within a file structure on your iPad, e.g. if you create a note in the Notes app, it is saved there, if you take a photo, it is saved in the Photos app. Content is usually also saved automatically when it is created, or edited, so you do not have to worry about saving it as you work on it.

Built-in Apps

The built-in iPad apps are the ones that appear on the Home screen when you turn on the iPad:

The iPad **Settings** app is another of the built-in apps and this is looked at in detail on pages 20-21.

- **App Store.** This can be used to access the App Store, from where additional apps can then be downloaded.

- **Calendar.** An app for storing appointments, important dates and other calendar information. It can be synced with iCloud.

- **Camera.** This gives direct access to the front-facing and rear-facing iPad cameras.

- **Clock.** This displays the current time and can be used to view the time in different countries and also as an alarm clock and a stopwatch.

- **Contacts.** An address book app. Once contacts are added here they can then also be accessed from other apps, such as Mail.

Some of the built-in apps, such as Mail and Contacts, interact with each other. However, since these are designed by Apple there is almost no chance of them containing viruses.

...cont'd

- **FaceTime.** This is an app that uses the built-in FaceTime camera on the iPad to hold video chats with other iPad users, or those with an iPhone, iPod Touch or a Mac computer.

- **Game Center.** For those who like gaming, this is an app for playing a variety of games, either individually or with friends.

- **iBooks.** This is an app for downloading electronic books, which can then be read on the iPad. This can be done for plain text or illustrated iBooks.

- **iTunes Store.** This app can be used to browse the iTunes store where music, TV shows, movies and more, can be downloaded to your iPad.

- **Mail.** This is the email app for sending and receiving email on your iPad.

- **Maps.** Use this app to view maps from around the world, find specific locations and get directions to destinations.

- **Messages.** This is the iPad messaging service, which can be used between iPads, iPhones, iPod Touches and Mac computers. It can be used with not only text but also photos and videos.

Beware

You need an Apple ID to obtain iBooks. They are downloaded in a matter of seconds and you cannot change your mind once you have entered your Apple ID details. For full details about obtaining an Apple ID, see page 89.

74

...cont'd

- **Music.** An app for playing music on your iPad and also viewing cover artwork. You can also use it to create your own playlists.

- **Newsstand.** Similar to iBooks, this app can be used to download and read newspapers and magazines.

Hot tip

It is worth investing in a good pair of headphones for listening to music so you do not disturb other people.

- **Notes.** If you need to jot down your thoughts or ideas, this app is perfect for just that.

- **Photo Booth.** A photography app that can be used to create distorted and special effects photos of people or objects.

- **Photos.** This is an app for viewing and editing photos and creating slideshows. It can also be used to share photos via iCloud.

- **Podcasts**. This can be used to download podcasts from within the App Store and then play them on your iPad.

Don't forget

A podcast is an audio, and sometimes video, program and they cover an extensive range of subjects.

- **Reminders.** Use this app for organization, when you want to create to-do lists and set reminders for events.

- **Safari.** The Apple web browser that has been developed for viewing the Web on your iPad.

- **Tips**. This can be used to display tips and hints for items on your iPad.

- **Videos.** This is an app for viewing videos on your iPad and also streaming them to a larger HDTV monitor.

Don't forget

The Tips and Podcasts apps are sometimes grouped together in a folder named Extras (see pages 84-85 for more information on folders).

75

For full details about obtaining an Apple ID, see page 89.

About the App Store

While the built-in apps that come with the iPad are flexible and versatile, it really comes into its own when you connect to the App Store. This is an online resource and there are thousands of apps there that can be downloaded and then used on your iPad, including categories from Lifestyle to Travel and Medical.

To use the App Store, you must first have an Apple ID. This can be obtained when you first connect to the App Store. Once you have an Apple ID you can start exploring the App Store:

1 Tap once on the **App Store** app on the Home screen

2 The latest available apps are displayed on the homepage of the App Store, including the Editor's Choice, featured in the top panel

3 Tap on these buttons to view the apps according to **Featured**, **Top Charts**, **Explore**, **Purchased** and **Updates**

...cont'd

Viewing apps

To view apps in the App Store and read about their content and functionality:

 Tap once on an app

 General details about the app are displayed

Don't forget

If it is an upgraded version of an app, this page will include details of any fixes and improvements that have been made.

 Swipe left or right here to view additional information about the app and view details

Reviews and related apps are available from the relevant buttons, next to the **Details** button

Finding Apps

Featured

Within the App Store, apps are separated into categories according to type. This enables you to find apps according to particular subjects. To do this:

Some apps will differ depending on the geographical location from where you are accessing the App Store.

With iOS 8 you can buy bundles of apps from the same developer, at a reduced price.

1 Tap once on the **Featured** button on the toolbar at the bottom of the App Store

2 Scroll left and right to view different category headings

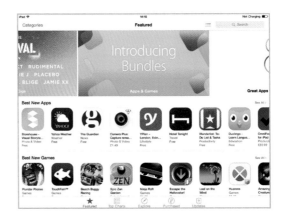

3 Scroll up the page to view additional categories and **Quick Links**

Top Charts
To find the top rated apps:

Tap once on the **Top Charts** button on the toolbar at the bottom of the App Store

The top overall paid for, free and top grossing apps are displayed

To find the top apps in different categories, tap once on this button

Tap once on a category

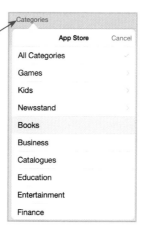

The top apps for that category are displayed

Beware

Do not limit yourself to just viewing the top apps. Although these are the most popular, there are also a lot of excellent apps within each category.

...cont'd

Explore

This is a feature which suggests a range of possible apps, some based on your geographic location. To use this:

Don't forget

To turn on Location Services for the App Store, go to **Settings > Privacy > Location Services** and tap once on the **App Store** button. Under **Allow Location Access** tap once on the **While Using the App** option.

1 Tap once on the **Explore** button on the toolbar at the bottom of the App Store

2 Tap once on the **Allow** button to enable the App Store to use your location (**Location Services** has to be turned On)

Allow "App Store" to access your location while you use the app?
Your location is used to find relevant apps nearby.

Don't Allow   Allow

3 Recommendations will appear in the **Explore** window, with category options in the left-hand panel

Don't forget

In the top of the Explore window is a **Popular Near Me** section that highlights apps that are relevant to your location.

4 Tap once on one of the categories to view specific apps for these

Searching for apps

Another way to find apps is with the App Store Search box,
which is located at the top-right corner of the App Store
window. To use this:

 Tap once in the **Search**
box to bring up the iPad
virtual keyboard

For more information
about using the iPad
virtual keyboard see
Chapter Three.

2 Enter a search keyword
or phrase

3 Suggested apps appear as
you are typing

4 Tap once on an app
to view it

Obtaining and Updating Apps

When you identify an app that you would like to use, it can be downloaded to your iPad. To do this:

Apps usually download in a few minutes, or less, depending on the speed of your Wi-Fi connection.

Some apps have 'in-app purchases'. This is additional content that has to be paid for when it is downloaded.

1 Find the app you want to download and tap once on the button next to the app (this will say Free or will have a price)

2 The button changes to show **Install**. Tap on this once

3 Enter your Apple ID details and tap once on the **OK** button

4 The app will begin to download on your iPad

5 Once the app is downloaded tap once on it to open and use it

Updating Apps

The world of apps is a dynamic and fast-moving one and new apps are being created and added to the App Store on a daily basis. Existing apps are also being updated, to improve their performance and functionality. Once you have installed an app from the App Store it is possible to obtain updates, at no extra cost (if the app was paid for). To do this:

1 When an update is available it is denoted by a red icon on the App Store app, showing how many updates are available

You should keep your apps as up-to-date as possible to take advantage of software fixes and any updates to the iPad operating system (iOS).

2 Tap once on the **App Store** app

3 In the App Store, tap once on the **Updates** button

 The available updates are displayed

5 Tap once on the button next to an app to update it

 Tap once on the **Update All** button to update all of the required apps

Update All

It is possible to set updates to apps to be downloaded automatically: **Settings > iTunes & App Store > Automatic Downloads**. Drag the buttons to On for the required items.

Organizing Apps

When you start downloading apps you will probably soon find that you have dozens, if not hundreds, of them. You can move between screens to view all of your apps by swiping left or right with one finger.

Hot tip

To move an app between screens, tap and hold on it until it starts to jiggle and a cross appears in the corner. Then drag it to the side of the screen. If there is space on the next screen the app will be moved there.

As more apps are added it can become hard to find the apps you want, particularly if you have to swipe between several screens. However, it is possible to organize apps into individual folders to make using them more manageable. To do this:

 Press on an app until it starts to jiggle and a white cross appears at the top-left corner

 Drag the app over another one

3 A folder is created, containing the two apps

4 The folder is given a default name, usually based on the category of the apps

5 Tap on the folder name and type a new name if required

6 Click the **Home** button once to finish creating the folder

7 Click the **Home** button again to return to the Home screen (this is done whenever you want to return to the Home screen from an apps folder)

8 The folder is added on the Home screen. Tap once on this to access the items within it

Beware

Only top-level folders can be created, i.e. sub-folders cannot be created. Also, one folder cannot be placed within another.

Hot tip

If you want to rename an apps folder after it has been created, tap and hold on it until it starts to jiggle. Then tap on it once and edit the folder name as in Step 5.

Deleting Apps

If you decide that you do not want certain apps anymore, they can be deleted from your iPad. However, they remain in the iCloud so that you can reinstall them if you change your mind. This also means that if you delete an app by mistake you can get it back from the App Store without having to pay for it again. To do this:

Beware

If you delete an app it will also delete any data that has been compiled with that app, even if you reinstall it from the App Store.

Don't forget

You cannot delete any of the built-in iPad apps, even by mistake.

 Press on an app until it starts to jiggle and a white cross appears at the top-left corner

 Tap once on the white cross to delete the app. In the Delete dialog box, tap once on the **Delete** button

Delete "Pages"

Deleting "Pages" will also delete all of its data from this iPad. Any documents & data stored in iCloud will not be deleted and can be managed in Settings.

Delete   Cancel

 Tap once on the **App Store** app

App Store

 Tap once on the **Purchased** button

Purchased

5 Apps that have been deleted have this iCloud icon next to them

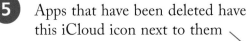

Pages
Apple
Version 2.0.1

 Tap once on the **iCloud** button to reinstall an app

5 Keeping in Touch

This chapter shows how to use your iPad to keep ahead in the fast-moving world of online communications, using email, social media, video calls and texting.

Getting Online

iPads can be used for a variety of different communications, but they all require online access. This is done via Wi-Fi and you will need to have an Internet Service Provider and a Wi-Fi router to connect to the Internet. Once this is in place you will be able to connect to a Wi-Fi network.

Don't forget

If you have the 4G version of the iPad you can obtain Internet access this way, but this has to be done through a provider of this service, as with a cell/mobile phone.

Don't forget

If you are connecting to your home Wi-Fi network the iPad should connect automatically each time, after it has been set up. If you are connecting in a public Wi-Fi area you will be asked which network you would like to join.

1 Tap once on the **Settings** app

Settings

2 Tap once on the **Wi-Fi** tab

🛜 Wi-Fi — Not Connected

3 Ensure the **Wi-Fi** button is in the **On** position

Wi-Fi

4 Available networks are shown here. Tap once on one to select it

CHOOSE A NETWORK...
NETGEAR
virginmedia6249958
Diagnostic Mode

5 Enter a password for your Wi-Fi router

Enter the password for "NETGEAR"
Cancel   **Enter Password**   Join

Password   ••••••••

6 Tap once on the **Join** button   Join

7 Once a network has been joined, a tick appears next to it. This now provides access to the Internet

Wi-Fi

✓ NETGEAR

Obtaining an Apple ID

An Apple ID is a registered email address and password with Apple that enables you to log in and use a variety of online Apple services. These include:

- App Store
- iTunes Store
- iCloud
- iMessage
- FaceTime
- Game Center
- iBooks

It is free to register for an Apple ID and this can be done when you access one of the apps or services which requires this, or you can do it on the Apple website at My Apple ID (**https://appleid.apple.com**)

If you are using an Apple ID to buy items, such as from iTunes or the App Store, you will need to provide a valid method of payment.

1   Tap once on the **Create an Apple ID** button

> Create an Apple ID

2   Enter your email address and a password

> **Create an Apple ID.**
>
> **Choose an Apple ID and password.**
> Enter your primary email address as your Apple ID. This will be used as the contact email address for your account. Please note that this email address must be verified before you can use certain Apple services.
>
> Apple ID   @mac.com
>
> Password   ....
>
> Confirm Password   ....
>
> **Create a security question.**
> Select a security question or create one of your own. This question will help us verify your identity should you forget your password.

My Apple ID is where you can access your Apple ID details and edit them, if required.

3   Enter additional details and enter the security code and tap once on the **Create Apple ID** button

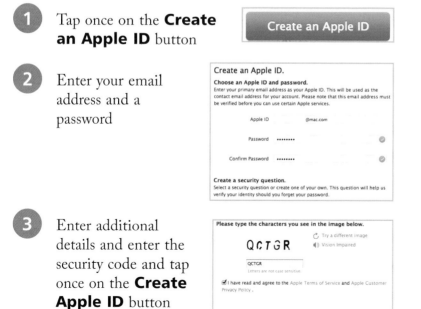

> Please type the characters you see in the image below.
>
>   Try a different image
>   Vision Impaired
>
> QCTGR
>
> QCTGR
> Letters are not case sensitive.
>
> ☑ I have read and agree to the Apple Terms of Service and Apple Customer Privacy Policy .
>
> Cancel   Create Apple ID

Setting up an Email Account

Email accounts

Email settings can be specified within the Settings app. Different email accounts can also be added there.

Hot tip

If you don't already have an email account set up, you can choose one of the providers from the list and you will be guided through the setup process. You may also find our title, **Internet for Seniors in easy steps** useful.

Hot tip

If your email provider is not on the **Add Account** list, tap once on **Other** at the bottom of the list and complete the account details using the information from your email provider.

1 Tap once on the **Settings** app

2 Tap once on the **Mail, Contacts, Calendars** link

Mail, Contacts, Calendars

3 Tap once on the **Add Account** link to add a new account

ACCOUNTS

iCloud
Mail, Contacts, Calendars, Safari, Reminders, Notes, Photos, Find My iPad and 2 more... >

Add Account >

4 Tap once on the type of email account you want to add

< Mail, Contacts...   **Add Account**

iCloud

Exchange

Google

YAHOO!

5 Enter the details for the account. Tap once on the **Next** button

Cancel	**Gmail**	Next
Name	Nick Vandome	
Email	nickvandome@googlemail.com	
Password	••••••••	
Description	nickvandome@googlemail.com	

6 Drag these buttons **On** or **Off** to specify which functions are to be available for the required account

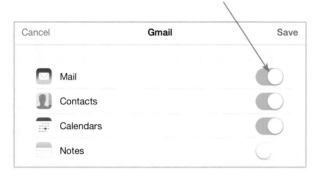

If you set up more than one email account, messages from all of them can be downloaded and displayed by **Mail**.

7 Each new account is added under the **Accounts** heading of the Mail, Contacts, Calendars section

ACCOUNTS

iCloud
Mail, Contacts, Calendars, Safari, Reminders, Notes, Photos, Find My iPad and 2 more…

nickvandome@googlemail.com
Mail, Contacts, Calendars

Add Account

Email settings

Email settings can be specified within the Settings app. Different email accounts can also be added there.

1 Under the Mail section there are several options for how Mail operates and looks. These include the number of messages being displayed, previewing emails and font size

MAIL	
Preview	2 Lines >
Show To/Cc Label	
Flag Style	Color >
Ask Before Deleting	
Load Remote Images	
Organize By Thread	
Always Bcc Myself	
Mark Addresses	Off >
Increase Quote Level	On >
Signature	Sent from my iPad >

The Threads option can be turned On to show connected email conversations within your Inbox. If there is a thread of emails this is indicated by this symbol. Tap on it once to view the thread.

Emailing

Email on the iPad is created, sent and received using the Mail app. This provides a range of functionality for managing email, including adding mailboxes and viewing email conversation threads.

Accessing Mail

To access Mail and start sending and receiving emails:

Hot tip

To quickly delete an email from your Inbox, swipe on it from right to left and tap once on the **Trash** button. This also generates options to **Flag** the email and a **More** button, from which you can reply, forward, mark or move the current email.

 Tap once on the **Mail** app (the red icon in the corner displays the number of unread emails in your Inbox)

 Tap once on a message to display it in the main panel

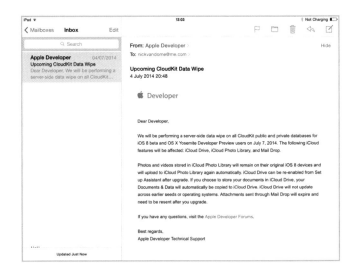

Don't forget

If the **Fetch New Data** option in the **Mail, Contacts, Calendar** Setting is set to **Push**, new emails will be downloaded automatically from your mail server. To check manually for new downloads, swipe down from the top of the mailbox pane.

 Use these buttons to, from left to right, flag a message, move a message, delete a message, respond to a message and create a new message

...cont'd

4 Tap once on this button to reply to a message, forward it to a new recipient, save an image in a message or print it

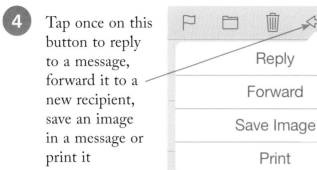

Reply

Forward

Save Image

Print

Creating email

To create and send an email:

Hot tip

Images in an email can also be saved by tapping and holding on them and then tapping once on the **Save Image** button.

1 Tap once on this button to create a new message

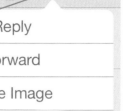

2 Enter a recipient name in the To box, or tap on one of the suggestions to select it

To: eilidh

To

Recent
other **eilidh**@mac.com

Eildih Vandome
home **eilidh**vandome@mac.com

Hot tip

If the recipient is included in your Contacts app, their details will appear as you type. Tap once on the email address, if it appears, to include it in the **To** field.

3 Enter a subject

Subject: **Lunch tomorrow?**

4 Enter the body text

Subject: Lunch tomorrow?

Hi, would you like to have lunch tomorrow?

Sent from my iPad

5 Tap once on the **Send** button to send the email to the recipient

Send

...cont'd

Mailboxes

Different categories of email messages can be managed via Mailboxes. For instance, you may want to keep your social emails separately from ones that apply to financial activities.

Hot tip

Messages can be edited within individual mailboxes. To do this, select a mailbox and tap once on the **Edit** button. The message can then be edited with the **Delete**, **Move** or **Mark** options at the bottom of the window.

Don't forget

One mailbox that can be included is for VIPs, i.e. your most important contacts. To add these from an email, tap and hold on the person's name in an email you receive from them and tap once on the **Add to VIP** button. Under **Mailboxes**, tap once on **VIP** to view emails from all of your VIPs.

 From your Inbox, tap once on the **Mailboxes** button

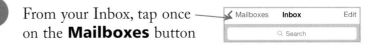

2 The current mailboxes are displayed. Tap once on the **Edit** button

3 Tap once on the **New Mailbox** button at the bottom of the Mailboxes panel

New Mailbox

4 Enter a name for the new mailbox. Tap once on the **Save** button

5 Tap once on the **Done** button

Done

6 To delete a mailbox, tap on it under **Edit Mailbox**, then tap once on the **Delete Mailbox** button

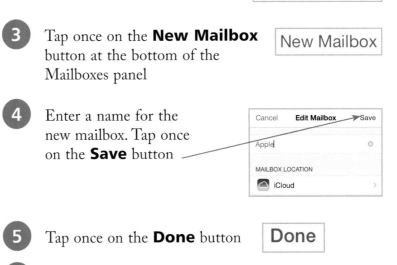

Adding Social Media

Using social media sites such as Facebook, Twitter and Flickr to keep in touch with families and friends has now become common across all generations. On the iPad with iOS 8 it is possible to link to these accounts so that you can share content to them from your iPad and also view updates through the Notification Center and Safari. To do this:

1. Tap once on the **Settings** app

2. Select the required social networking option in the left-hand panel

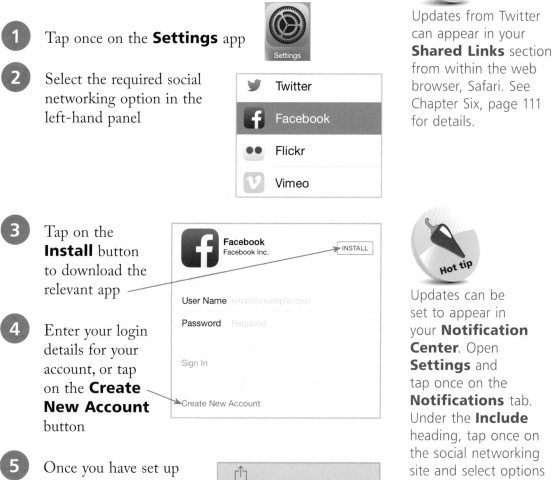

Updates from Twitter can appear in your **Shared Links** section from within the web browser, Safari. See Chapter Six, page 111 for details.

3. Tap on the **Install** button to download the relevant app

4. Enter your login details for your account, or tap on the **Create New Account** button

Updates can be set to appear in your **Notification Center**. Open **Settings** and tap once on the **Notifications** tab. Under the **Include** heading, tap once on the social networking site and select options for how you would like the notifications to appear.

5. Once you have set up your account, tap on the **Share** button, where it is available, to share content with your social networking sites

Text Messaging

Text messaging should not be thought of as the domain of the younger generation. On your iPad you can join the world of text with the Apple iMessage service that is accessed via the Messages app. This enables text, photo, video and audio messages to be sent, free of charge, between users of iOS (version 5 onwards), on the iPad, iPhone and iPod Touch. iMessages can be sent to cell/mobile phone numbers and email addresses. To use iMessages:

Beware

If a number, or an email address, is not recognized it shows up in red in the **To** box.

 Tap once on the **Messages** app

 You have to sign in with your Apple ID before you can use Messages. Enter these details and tap on the **Sign In** button

iMessage

iMessages can be sent between iPhone, iPad, iPod touch, and Mac.
Learn more about iMessage

Apple ID   nickvandome@mac.com

Password

Sign In

 Tap once on this button to create a new message and start a new conversation

 Tap once on this button to select someone from your contacts

5 Tap once on a contact to select them as the recipient of the new message

Groups	**All Contacts**
Q Search	

V

Eilidh **Vandome**

Lucy **Vandome**

Mark **Vandome**

Mike **Vandome**

Creating iMessages

To create and edit messages and conversations:

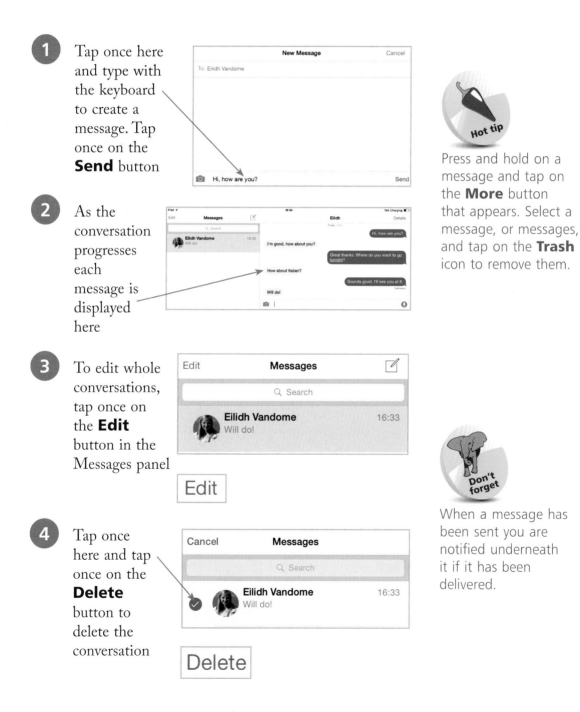

1 Tap once here and type with the keyboard to create a message. Tap once on the **Send** button

2 As the conversation progresses each message is displayed here

3 To edit whole conversations, tap once on the **Edit** button in the Messages panel

4 Tap once here and tap once on the **Delete** button to delete the conversation

Hot tip

Press and hold on a message and tap on the **More** button that appears. Select a message, or messages, and tap on the **Trash** icon to remove them.

Don't forget

When a message has been sent you are notified underneath it if it has been delivered.

...cont'd

Sending Photos and Videos

Within Messages in iOS 8 it is possible to add different types of media to a text message, including photos and videos. To do this:

Don't forget

If you do not like a photo or video that you have taken, tap once on the **Retake** button and try again.

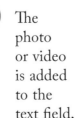

1 To add a photo or a video, tap once on the camera icon next to the text field. Select an item from your **Photo Library** or take a photo or video

2 The Camera app opens. Select the photo or video option and capture by tapping on the shutter button

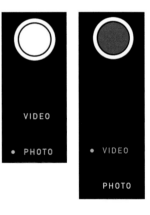

3 Tap once on the **Use Photo** or **Use Video** button

4 The photo or video is added to the text field, where new text can also be added

Adding Audio Clips

You can also send family and friends audio messages in an iMessage so that they can hear from you to. To do this:

 Press and hold on the microphone icon at the right-hand side of the text field

 Create your audio clip and tap once here to send it

 Tap once here to delete the current clip and start recording again

Sending your location

With Messages you can now also show people your location (by sending a map) rather than just telling them. To do this:

1 Once a conversation has started, tap once on the **Details** button

Details

2 Tap once on the **Send My Current Location**, or **Share My Location** buttons

| LOCATION |
| Send My Current Location |
| Share My Location |

3 For Share My Location, tap once on one of the options for how long you want your location to be shared for

Share for One Hour

Share Until End of Day

Share Indefinitely

Hot tip

If you select **Share My Location**, this will be updated if your location changes (as long as Location Services is turned On, **Settings > Privacy > Location Services**).

Having a Video Chat

Video chatting is a very personal and interactive way to keep in touch with family and friends around the world. The FaceTime app provides this facility with other iPad, iPhone and iPod Touch users, or a Mac computer with FaceTime. To use FaceTime for video chatting:

 Tap once on the **FaceTime** app

 Recent video chats are shown under the Video tab. Tap once here to select a contact

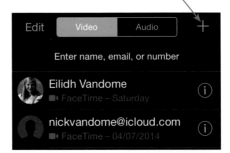

3 Tap once on a contact to access their details for making a FaceTime call

4 Tap once on their phone number or email address to make a FaceTime call. The recipient must have FaceTime on their iPad, iPhone, iPod Touch or Mac computer

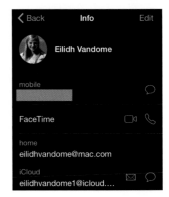

5 Once you
have selected
a contact,
FaceTime starts
connecting to
them and displays this at the top of the screen

Eilidh Vandome
FaceTime...

6 When you have connected, your contact appears in
the main window and you appear in a picture-in-
picture thumbnail in the corner

7 Tap once on this button to swap
between cameras on your iPad

8 Tap once on this button to end the
FaceTime call

9 If someone else makes a call to you, tap
once on the **Decline** or **Accept** buttons

Hot tip

The contacts for
FaceTime calls are
taken from the iPad
Contacts app (see
page 120). You can
also add new contacts
directly to the contacts
list by tapping once on
the + sign and adding
the relevant details for
the new contact.

Communication Apps

Within the App Store there is a range of communication apps that can be used to contact friends and family via text, phone and video. There are also several apps for sharing information, updates and photos. Some of these are:

- **Facebook.** The social networking phenomenon that has over a billion users around the world. This app enables you to create and use a Facebook account from your iPad. You can then interact with friends and family by posting messages, comments and photos.

- **Twitter.** Another one of the top social networking sites on the Web. It provides the facility to post text or news messages of up to 140 characters. You can choose other users to follow, so you see their messages (Tweets) and other people can follow you too.

- **Flickr.** An iPad version of the popular photo- and video-sharing site. You have to register and once you have done this you can share your photos and videos with a vast online community.

- **Pictures with Words.** Another photo-sharing app that enables you to share your photos online and also add captions, text and graphics to your images.

- **WordPress.** A web publishing app that can be used to create online blogs and also your own websites.

- **Gmail.** If you have a Gmail account this will enable you to access it directly from your iPad.

- **Windows Live Hotmail.** This can be used to access email from a Hotmail (or MSN or Live) account.

- **Yahoo! Messenger.** This app is similar to Skype in that it offers free video and voice calling to other Yahoo! Messenger users.

- **Talkatone for Google Voice and Facebook.** Another app for free phone calls and texts to phones in the USA and Canada.

6 On a Web Safari

This chapter shows how to use the functionality of the built-in iPad web browser, Safari, to access the Web and start enjoying the benefits of the online world.

Around Safari

The Safari app is the default web browser on the iPad. This can be used to view web pages, save favorites and read pages with the Reader function. To start using Safari:

 Tap once on the **Safari** app

 Tap once on the Address Bar at the top of the Safari window. Type a web page address

When you tap in the Address Bar you also have the option for opening a page by tapping on one of the icons which appear in the Favorites window below the Address Bar. See page 108 for more details about this.

As you type in the Address Bar the options and suggestions below it become more defined.

3 Tap once on the **Go** button on the keyboard to open the web page, or select one of the options below the Address Bar

Go

4 The selected page opens with the top toolbar visible. As you scroll down the page this disappears to give you a greater viewing area. Tap on the top of the screen or scroll back up to display the toolbar again

…cont'd

5 Swipe up and down and left and right to navigate around the page

When a page opens in Safari a blue status bar underneath the Address Bar indicates the progress of the loading page.

6 Swipe outwards with thumb and forefinger to zoom in on a web page (pinch inwards to zoom back out)

Double-tap with one finger to zoom in on a page by a set amount. Double-tap with one finger to return to normal view. If the page has been zoomed by a greater amount by pinching, double-tap with two fingers to return to normal view.

Beware

Don't use **Autofill** for names and passwords for any sites with sensitive information, such as banking sites, if other people have access to the iPad.

Hot tip

If the **Open New Tabs in Background** is set to On, you can tap and hold on a link on a web page and select **Open in New Tab**. The link then opens in a new tab behind the one you are viewing.

Don't forget

Cookies are small items from websites that obtain details from your browser when you visit a site. The cookie remembers the details for the next time you visit the site.

Safari Settings

Settings for Safari can be specified in the Settings app.

1 Open the Settings app and tap once on the **Safari** tab

Safari

2 Tap once on the **Search Engine** link to select a default search engine to use

Search Engine

3 Tap once here for options for filling in online forms

Passwords & AutoFill

4 Drag this button to **On** to open new pages in the background of your current page

Open New Tabs in Background

5 Drag this button to **On** to keep the Favorites Bar in view under the Address Bar in Safari

Show Favorites Bar

6 Tap once on the **Block Cookies** link to specify how Safari deals with cookies from websites

Block Cookies

7 Tap once on **Clear History and Website Data** to remove these

Clear History and Website Data

8 Drag this button to **On** to enable alerts for when you visit a fraudulent website

Fraudulent Website Warning

9 Drag this button to **On** to block pop-up messages

Block Pop-ups

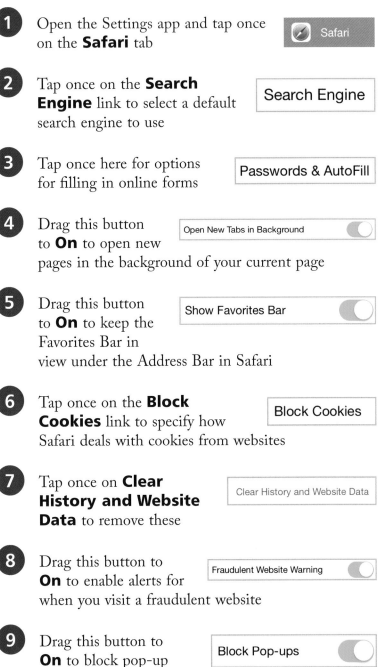

Navigating Pages

When you are viewing pages within Safari there are a number of functions that can be used:

 Tap once on these buttons to move forward and back between web pages that have been visited

2 Tap once here to view Bookmarked pages, Reading List pages and Shared Links

Tap once here to add a bookmark, add to a reading list, add an icon to your iPad Home screen, email a link to a page, Tweet a page, send it to Facebook or print a page

4 Tap once here to add a new tab

 Tap once on a link on a page to open it. Tap and hold to access additional options, to open in a new tab, add to a Reading List or copy the link

Tap and hold on an image and tap once on **Save Image** or **Copy**

Tap and hold on the **Forward** and **Back** buttons to view lists of previously-visited pages in these directions.

See page 110 for more on bookmarking.

If a web page has this button in the Address/Search box it means that the page can be viewed with the **Reader** function. This displays the page as text only, without any of the accompanying design to distract from the content. Tap on the button so that it turns black to activate the Reader.

Opening New Tabs

Safari supports tabbed browsing, which means that you can open separate pages within the same window and access them by tapping on each tab at the top of the page:

The items that appear in the Favorites window can be determined within **Settings > Safari** and tapping once on the **Favorites** link.

1 Tap once here to open a new tab for another page

2 Open a new page by entering a web address into the Address Bar, or tap on one of the thumbnails in the **Favorites** window

3 Tap once on the tab headings to move between tabbed pages

4 Tap once on the cross at the top of a tab to close it

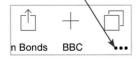

Hot tip

If there are too many items to be displayed on the Favorites Bar, tap once on this button to view the other items.

Tab View

A previous feature of the iOS operating system on the iPhone was the ability to view all of your open Safari tabs on one screen. In iOS 8 this functionality has also come to the iPad with Tab View. To use this:

1 Tap once here to activate Tab View

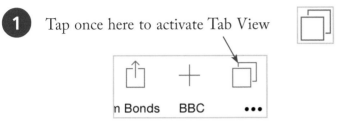

2 All of the currently open tabs are displayed. Tap once on one to open it

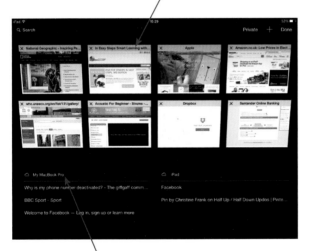

3 If you have open Safari tabs on other Apple devices, these will shown at the bottom of the window

4 Tap once on this button at the top of the window to open another tab

5 Tap once on this button to open a **Private** tab, where no browsing record will be recorded during this browsing session

Hot tip

Tab View can also be activated by pinching inwards with thumb and forefinger on a web page that is at normal magnification, i.e. 1 to 1.

Don't forget

Tap once on the **Done** button at the top of the Tab View window to exit this and return to the web page that was being viewed when Tab View was activated.

Bookmarking Pages

Once you start using Safari you will soon build up a collection of favorite pages that you visit regularly. To access these quickly they can be bookmarked so that you can then go to them in one tap. To set up and use bookmarks:

Don't forget

The Favorites Bar appears underneath the Address Bar in Safari. This includes items that have been added as bookmarks.

1 Open a web page that you want to bookmark. Tap once here to access the sharing options

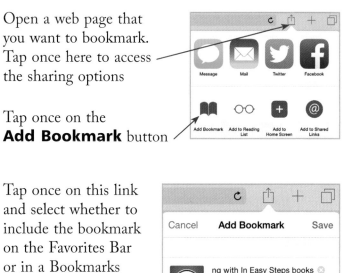

2 Tap once on the **Add Bookmark** button

3 Tap once on this link and select whether to include the bookmark on the Favorites Bar or in a Bookmarks folder

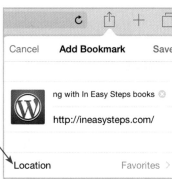

4 Tap once on the **Save** button

5 Tap once here to view all of the bookmarks. The Bookmarks folders are listed. Tap once on the **Edit** button at the bottom of the panel to delete or rename the folders

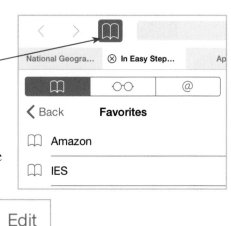

Edit

Reading List and Shared Links

The button in Step 5 on the previous page can be used to access your Reading List and Shared Links.

Reading List

This is a list of web pages that have been saved for reading at a later date. The great thing about this function is that the pages can be read even when you are offline and not connected to the Internet.

Tap on this button to view your **Reading List**

Reading List items can be added from the Share button in Step 1 on the previous page.

Shared Links

If you have added a Twitter account on your iPad you will be able to view your updates from the Shared Links button.

Tap on this button to view your **Shared Links** updates

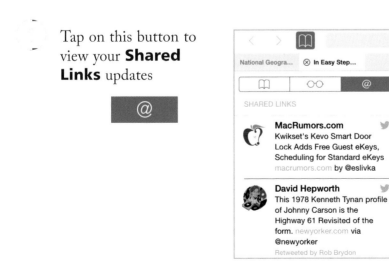

If you have accounts with Facebook or Twitter, you can link to these from the left-hand panel of the **Settings** app. Once you have done this you can share content to these sites from apps on your iPad.

Web Apps

Although Safari can comfortably meet all of your web browsing needs, there are a number of other browser apps that can be downloaded from the App Store. Generally, they have similar functionality but each has its own features too. It is worth looking at a few to compare the different interfaces. Some to try are:

- **Atomic Web Browser.** This is a browser that has a full-screen view, one-touch tabbed browsing and also a wider range of Multi-Touch Gestures for navigating.

- **Dolphin Browser.** This browser has four different search engines from which to choose and Gestures and Sidebars for accessing pages quickly.

- **Flash Video Web Browser.** This is an iPad browser with the unique feature of being able to play Flash video files. It does this by processing the content on its own servers and then sending it back to the browser. It is invaluable if you want to watch a lot of Flash video.

- **Mercury Browser.** A stylish browser which includes customizable themes, ten-tab browsing, full-screen view and effective download options for links or images.

- **Opera Mini Web Browser.** This is a fast browser that compresses data before downloading it for viewing. One of the fastest browsers available for the iPad.

Beware

Flash is a video and animation format that is used widely on the Web. However, Flash video files cannot usually be played on the iPad.

Don't forget

There is also the **Chrome** app in the App Store, which is an iPad version of the popular web browser produced by Google.

7 Staying Organized

Taking Notes

It is always useful to have a quick way of making notes of everyday things, such as shopping lists, recipes or packing lists for traveling. On your iPad the Notes app is perfect for this function. To use it:

1 Tap once on the **Notes** app

2 Tap once on the note to access the keyboard. Start writing the note

Don't forget

Text in a note can be edited in the same way as any other text document.

3 Tap once on this button on the keyboard to hide the keyboard and finish the note. To edit an existing note, tap once on the text and the keyboard will reappear

4 As the note is created it appears in the Notes panel. The most recent note is at the top and the first line of the note is the title. Tap once on a note to view it

‹ Accounts	
My shopping list	
My packing list	15:55
Menu list	15:55

Tap once on this button to create a new note

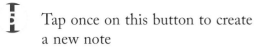

Tap once on this button to delete the current note

Tap once on this button to share (via Message, Mail, Twitter or Facebook), copy or print a note

Sending notes to iCloud

If you are using iCloud this can be used to send your notes to your iCloud account. To do this:

Access the Settings app and tap once on the **iCloud** link

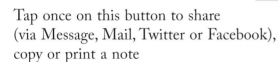

iCloud
nickvandome@mac.com

Drag the **Notes** button to **On**

Notes

In the Notes app, tap once on the **Accounts** button

iPad 🔋		
‹ Accounts		
iPad Seniors iOS 8	12:54	31 July 2014 12:54
		iPad Seniors iOS 8
iPad iOS 8	Yesterday	

The different accounts are listed, including **iCloud**. Those under **On My iPad** are only stored on your iPad and not in the iCloud. New folders can be added under the iCloud section, but this can only be done within Notes on a Mac computer

Accounts	
All Notes	›
ON MY IPAD	
Notes	›
ICLOUD	
All iCloud	›
New Folder	›
New Folder 2	›

Beware

If iCloud is set up for Notes then all of your notes will appear under the **All Notes** heading under **Accounts**. Once in a specific account each note stays there, where it was created.

Beware

If you turn off Notes in iCloud the Accounts option will not be available and your notes will only be stored on your iPad.

Reminders are one of the items that can also be viewed through the online iCloud service, which is provided once you have an Apple ID. This is accessed at **www.icloud.com** The other items that can be accessed there include Contacts, Calendar and Notes.

If Family Sharing has been set up (see pages 42-45 for details of this) you can also create a family reminder that will appear for all members in your family sharing circle. To do this, tap once on the **Family** (Sharing with) button and add a reminder in the usual way.

Setting Reminders

Another useful organization app is Reminders. This enables you to create lists for different topics and then set reminders for specific items. A date and time can be set for each reminder and, when this is reached, the reminder appears on your iPad screen. To use Reminders:

1 Tap once on **Reminders** app

2 The Reminder lists are located in the left-hand panel. Tap once on the **New List** button for a list, or **Reminders** to create a new reminder

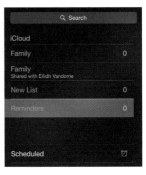

3 Tap once on a new line and enter the reminder

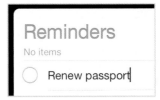

4 Hide the keyboard and tap once on the **i** button to access the **Details** window

5 Drag this button to **On**

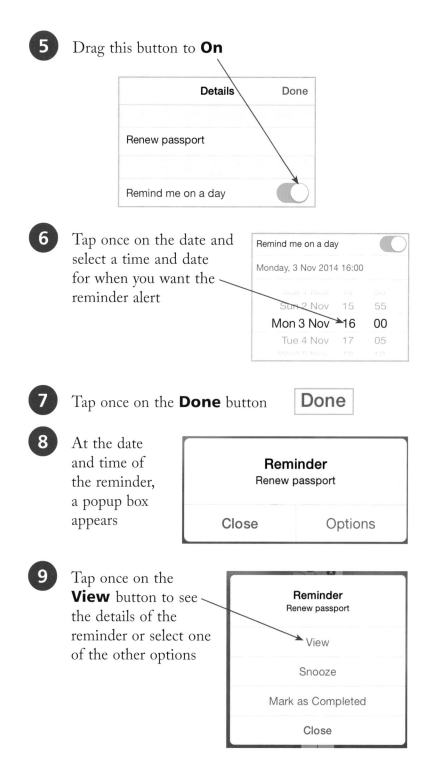

Details	Done
Renew passport	
Remind me on a day	⬤

6 Tap once on the date and select a time and date for when you want the reminder alert

Remind me on a day	⬤
Monday, 3 Nov 2014 16:00	
Sun 2 Nov	15	55
Mon 3 Nov	**16**	**00**
Tue 4 Nov	17	05

7 Tap once on the **Done** button

Done

8 At the date and time of the reminder, a popup box appears

Reminder
Renew passport

Close	Options

9 Tap once on the **View** button to see the details of the reminder or select one of the other options

Reminder
Renew passport

View

Snooze

Mark as Completed

Close

Hot tip

For a recurring reminder, tap once on the **Repeat** link in the **Details** window (if **Remind me on a day** is On) and select a repeat option from Never, Every Day, Every Week, Every 2 Weeks, Every Month, Every Year. The reminder will then appear at the specified timescale, at the time set in Step 6.

Don't forget

Set the time and date for reminders by dragging up and down on the relevant barrels within the **Details** window. The time can be set in five-minute intervals.

Using the Calendar

The built-in iPad Calendar can be used to create and view appointments and events. To do this:

The iPad calendar uses continuous scrolling to move through Month view. This means you can view weeks across different months, rather than just viewing each month in its entirety, i.e. you can view the second half of one month and the first half of the next one in the same calendar window.

 1 Tap once on the **Calendar** app

 2 By default the calendar is displayed in a month view. Swipe up and down to move between the weeks and months

 3 Tap once here to view the calendar by Day, Week, Month or Year view. Swipe left or right to move between days, weeks, months or years

4 Tap once on the **Today** button to view the current date. Tap once on the bar to move between dates

5 Tap once on this button to create a new event, or press and hold on a different date to add an event here

$+$

Drag the **All-day** button to **On** to set the event for the whole day.

All-day

 6 Enter a Title and a Location for the event

 7 Drag the **All-day** button from **On** to **Off** to set a timescale for the event

Cancel	New Event	Add
Family party		
Edinburgh		
All-day		
Starts	3 Nov 2014	15:00
Ends		22:00

...cont'd

8 Tap on the **Starts** and **Ends** dates to set these. Tap once on the **Add** button

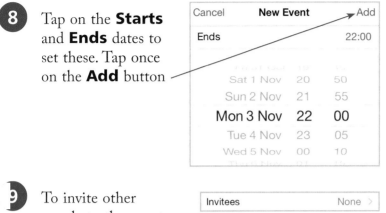

Hot tip

A new event can also be created in **Day** view. Tap and hold on a time slot to access the **Add Event** window.

9 To invite other people to the event, tap once on the **Invitees** link (Calendars needs to be On in iCloud for this function)

10 Tap once on this button to select a contact from your address book

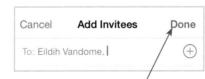

Hot tip

Tap once on the **Repeat** link in the **New Event** window to set a recurring event, such as a birthday. The repeat options are Every Day, Every Week, Every 2 Weeks, Every Month or Every Year.

11 The contact is added as an invitee for the event

12 Tap once on the **Done** button. An email invitation will then be sent to the recipient's email address

13 Press and hold on an event and tap on the **Edit** button to alter the details for the event

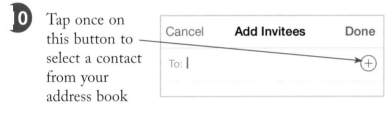

Don't forget

Swipe to the bottom of the **Edit Event** window to remove an event with the **Delete Event** button.

119

Your iPad Address Book

There is a built-in address book app on your iPad: Contacts. This enables you to store contact details which can then be used to contact people via email, iMessage or FaceTime. To add contacts:

1 Tap once on the **Contacts** app

2 Tap once on this button to add a new contact

3 Enter the required details for a contact

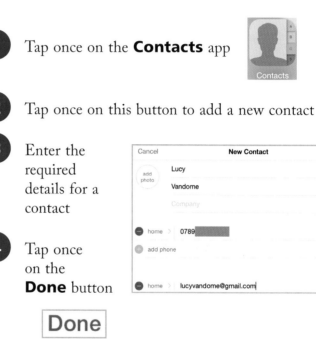

4 Tap once on the **Done** button

Done

5 Use these buttons to contact someone via text message (iMessage) or share their contact details

Send Message

Share Contact

6 Tap once on the **Edit** button to edit details in an individual entry

Edit

7 To delete a contact, swipe to the bottom of the window in Edit mode and tap once on the **Delete Contact** button

Delete Contact

Hot tip

Tap once on a contact's email address to go directly to Mail to send them an email. Tap once on a cell/ mobile phone number to access FaceTime for a video call (if the recipient has a compatible device and software for this).

Don't forget

Contact details of an individual can be shared via email or as an iMessage.

Keeping Notified

Although the Notification Center feature is not an app in its own right, it can be used to display information from a variety of apps. These appear as a list for all of the items you want to be reminded about or be made aware of. Notifications are set up within the Settings app. To do this:

Tap once on the **Settings** app

Tap once on the **Notifications** tab

In the **Include** section, tap on an item to determine how it operates when it displays a notification

Drag the **Allow Notifications** button to **On** to allow notifications to be displayed for this item

Make selections for how you want the notification to appear. This can include sound for the notifications, showing an app badge and also displaying the notification on the Lock Screen

Don't forget

The items that can be included in the **Today** view of the Notification Center are a summary of the relevant items for Today and Tomorrow and also the details from the current day in your Calendar and your Reminders.

...cont'd

Including Notifications
If you want to include more notifications from other apps this can also be done within the Notifications section of the Settings app:

1 Access the **Notifications** section of the Settings app, as shown on the previous page

2 Swipe down the page to the **Do Not Include** section. Tap once on the app that you want included for notifications

DO NOT INCLUDE

 Hotels.com

Hou Chronicle

Tabs HD

Better Homes

 Instagram

3 Tap on the **Show in Notification Center** button

❮ Notifications   Instagram

Allow Notifications

Show in Notification Center   None ❯

Sounds

Badge App Icon

Show on Lock Screen

Show alerts on the lock screen, and in Notification Center when it is accessed from the lock screen.

ALERT STYLE WHEN UNLOCKED

None   Banners   Alerts

Alerts require an action before proceeding.
Banners appear at the top of the screen and

4 Select the number of notifications that you want to be displayed for the selected app

❮ Instagram   Show in Notification Center

No Recent Items

1 Recent Item   ✓

5 Recent Items

10 Recent Items

20 Recent Items

Viewing Notifications

Once the Notifications settings have been selected, they can be used to keep up-to-date with all of your important appointments and reminders, via the Notification Center. It can also be used to display the weather for your current location. To view the Notification Center from any screen:

1 Drag down from the top of any screen to view the Notification Center. Tap on the **Today** button to view the Weather summary, Calendar items, Reminder items, and a summary of items for the next day

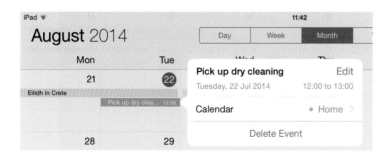

Press and hold on this button and swipe up to close the Notification Center:

2 Swipe up the page to view all of the items. Tap on one to open it in its own default app

...cont'd

 3 Swipe to the bottom of the **Today** page and tap once on the **Edit** button to specify the items that appear on this page

Edit

① New Widget Available

Don't forget

When an item has been removed in Step 4 it appears under Do Not Include and it can be reinstated from here by tapping on the green button that appears next to it.

 4 Tap once on the red circle next to an item to remove it from appearing on the Today page. Tap once on the **Done** button to return to the Today page

11:39   Not Charging
Today   Done

- Today Summary
- ⌖ Traffic Conditions
- Calendar
- Reminders
- Tomorrow Summary

5 Tap once on the **Notifications** button to view these items. As with the Today items, tap once on a notification to view it within its app

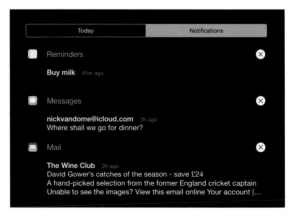

| Today | Notifications |

Reminders   ⊗
Buy milk 45m ago

Messages   ⊗
nickvandome@icloud.com 2h ago
Where shall we go for dinner?

Mail   ⊗
The Wine Club 2h ago
David Gower's catches of the season - save £24
A hand-picked selection from the former England cricket captain
Unable to see the images? View this email online Your account |...

Do Not Disturb

Although Notifications can be set so that you never miss a new message or alert, there may be times when you do not want to receive any calls or audio alerts. This can be done with the Do Not Disturb function.

1 Tap once on the **Settings** app

Tap once on the **Do Not Disturb** tab

Drag the **Scheduled** button to **On**, to specify a time period for when you do not want to be disturbed

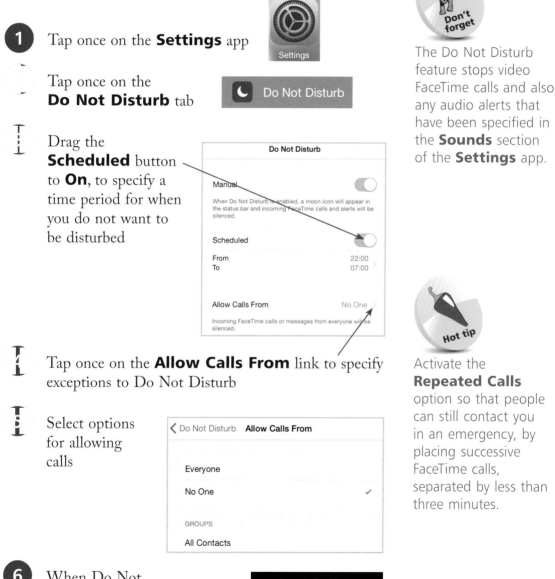

Tap once on the **Allow Calls From** link to specify exceptions to Do Not Disturb

Select options for allowing calls

6 When Do Not Disturb is activated, a half-moon appears at the top of the screen next to the time

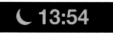

Don't forget

Most organization apps are found in the **Productivity** category of the App Store.

Beware

For handwriting to work most effectively in Bamboo Paper, **Multitasking Gestures** should be turned Off in the **General** section of the **Settings** app.

Organization Apps

In the App Store there is a wide range of organization apps for tasks such as note-taking. Some of these are:

- **Evernote.** One of the most popular note-taking apps. You can create individual notes and also save them into notebook folders. Evernote works across multiple devices so, if it is installed on other computers or mobile devices, you can access your notes wherever you are.

- **Popplet.** This is a note-taking app that enables you to link notes together, so you can form a mindmap-type creation. You can also include photos and draw pictures.

- **Dropbox.** This is an online service for storing and accessing files. You can upload files from your iPad and then access them from other devices with an Internet connection.

- **Bamboo Paper.** This is another note-taking app, but it allows you to do this by handwriting rather than typing. The free version comes with one notebook into which you can put your notes and the paid-for version provides another 20.

- **Errands To-Do List.** A virtual To-Do list that can help keep you organized and up-to-date. You can create your own folders for different items and have alerts remind you of important dates, events and items.

- **Notability.** Another app that utilizes handwriting for creating notes. It also accommodates word processing, and audio recording.

- **Alarmed.** An app for keeping you on time and up-to-date. It has an alarm clock, pop-up reminders and pop-up timers.

- **Grocery List.** Shopping need never be the same again with this virtual shopping list app.

- **World Calendar.** Find out public holiday information for 40 countries around the world.

Productivity Apps

If you want to do more than just use organization apps, there are some excellent productivity apps for creating word processing documents, presentations and spreadsheets. These can be used to write letters, produce holiday presentations or do household accounts. Some of the productivity apps are:

- **Pages.** This is a powerful word processing app that has been developed by Apple. It can be used to create and save documents which can then be printed or shared via email. There are a number of templates on which documents can be based. There is also a range of formatting and content options.

- **Keynote.** Another Apple productivity app, this is a presentation app that can be used to create slides that can then be run as a presentation.

- **Numbers.** This is the spreadsheet app that is part of the same suite as Pages and Keynote. Again, templates are provided or you can create your spreadsheets from scratch to keep track of expenditure or household bills. You can enter formulas into cells to perform simple, or complicated, calculations.

- **Smart Office 2.** This app can be used to create, edit and share Microsoft Office documents, such as Word, PowerPoint and Excel. It supports all Microsoft Office versions since 1997 and also allows viewing of a variety of image files and PDF files.

- **iA Writer.** A simple but effective word processing app. It creates documents that can be synchronized across other devices and also copied to iCloud or Dropbox.

- **Free Spreadsheet.** This is similar to Numbers and although it does not have the same range of functionality it is still an effective spreadsheet.

- **GoodReader for iPad.** This is an app for viewing PDF documents and large documents such as manuals or long books. It also has a facility for annotating items.

Pages, Keynote and Numbers are part of Apple's iWork suite of productivity apps. They are free to download from the App Store with compatible iOS 8 devices.

PDF stands for Portable Document Format which is a file format created by Adobe to enable documents to be shared across different platforms without losing their formatting.

Printing Items

Printing from an iPad has advantages and disadvantages. The advantage is that it is done wirelessly so you do not have to worry about connecting wires and cables to a printer. The disadvantage is that not all printers work with the iPad printing system.

AirPrint

Content from an iPad is printed using the AirPrint system that is part of the iOS 8 operating system. This is a wireless printing system that connects to your printer through your Wi-Fi network. However, not all printers are AirPrint-enabled so it may not work with your current printer.

AirPrint can print content from Safari, Mail, Photos, Pages, Keynote, Numbers and PDF documents in iBooks. Some third-party apps have AirPrint facilities but this depends on individual developers. To print items using AirPrint:

Check on the Apple website for a list of AirPrint-enabled printers.

Some developers offer third-party printing apps for the iPad. However, these work with varying degrees of success.

1. Tap once on the tools option and tap once on the **Print** link

2. Select a printer or, if it has already been set up, tap once on the **Print** button to print

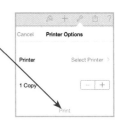

3. If your printer is not AirPrint compatible this will be shown in the **Printer** dialog box

8 Like a Good Book

Your iPad can be used for reading books, magazines and newspapers.

Newspapers and Magazines

With its portability and high-resolution Retina screen, the iPad is ideal for reading material, from magazines and newspapers to books. The former can be downloaded and read with the Newsstand app and the latter with the iBooks app. To access reading material with the Newsstand:

Don't forget

There is a wide range of newspapers available through the Newsstand, usually specific to your geographical location.

1 Tap once on the **Newsstand** app

2 The Newsstand bookcase is initially empty. Tap once on the **Store** button to access the Newsstand store

Newsstand — Store

Store

3 The Newsstand Store is incorporated within the App Store. Items can be found in the main featured panel or by swiping left and right between items underneath the top panel

Beware

The majority of magazines and newspapers are initially free to download. However, most then require a paid-for subscription once the initial trial period for the item has expired.

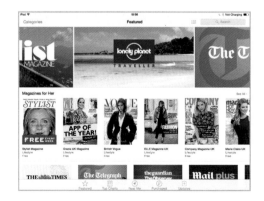

4 When you have found a suitable magazine, newspaper or journal, review and download it in the same way as with an app in the App Store

5 Downloaded items appear on the Newsstand bookcase (Library). Tap once on a cover to open that publication

Hot tip

If there is a red circle with a number in it on the Newsstand app, this indicates available updates for your existing publications.

Tap once on the **All Books** button in **My Books** and tap once on the **New Collection** button to create new shelves under specific headings. These can be used to store books according to genre. Swipe left and right to move between collections. To add books to a collection, tap once on the **Select** button and tap once on a book and then tap once on the **Move** button and tap once on the collection into which you want to move the selected item.

Books can be searched for in a similar way as for searching for apps. See page 81 for more details.

Finding Books

For anyone interested in reading, the iPad removes the need to carry around a lot of bulky books. Whether you are at home or traveling, you can keep hundreds of books on your iPad. This is done with the iBooks app, which can be used to download and read books across most genres; it is your own portable library. To use iBooks:

 Tap once on the **iBooks** app

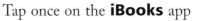 The iBooks app opens the iBooks Store at **My Books**, which consists of a bookcase, which initially

is empty, or displays items that you have already downloaded

Navigate through the iBooks Store in the same way as the App Store to find the required titles

Use the buttons on the bottom toolbar to search for items within the iBooks Store, under **Featured**, **Top Charts**, **Top Authors** and **Purchased**

Downloading Books

Once you have identified appropriate books they can then be downloaded to the **My Books** section of the iBooks app. To do this:

 Tap once on the book name or title to view its details

 View the details of the book and any reviews (under the **Reviews** heading)

 Tap once on this button to download a sample of the book

SAMPLE

 Tap once on the price (or Free) button to download the book

Under the **Related** heading in Step 2 you will find details of similar books to the one being viewed.

 Downloaded books appear in the **My Books** section of the iBooks app. Tap once on a book cover to open it and start reading

Reading Books

Reading an iBook

Once you have opened an iBook there are a number of ways to navigate and work with the content:

1 Tap once in the middle of a page in an iBook to access the top toolbar

2 Tap once on this button to return to the iBook **Library** (bookcase)

3 Tap once on this button to view the Table of Contents

4 Tap once on this button to change the text size

5 Tap once on this button to search for an item in the book

6 Tap once on this button to bookmark a page

7 Drag on this bottom bar to move through the book

Working with text

When you are reading an iBook there are a number of options for enhancing the reading experience, from looking up dictionary definitions of words, to making notes about the text. To do this:

 Tap and hold on a word to highlight it and access the text toolbar

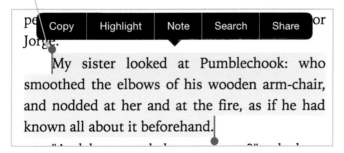 Tap once on the **Define** button to access a dictionary definition for the selected word. At the bottom of the window there are also options for searching the word over the Web

Beware

If you use the **Search Web** option in Step 2, this takes you away from the iBook page.

3 Highlight a word and drag on the blue dots to extend the highlighted area

...cont'd

4 Tap once on the **Highlight** button and select an option for how the text is highlighted

Highlight

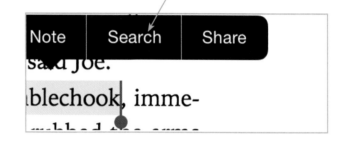

pearance ... e Joe, or Jorge."

My sister looked at Pumblechook: who smoothed the elbows of his wooden arm-chair, and nodded at her and at the fire, as if he had known all about it beforehand.

Beware

The more words you highlight for a search, the fewer results will be returned.

5 Highlight a word and tap on the **Search** button

Note | Search | Share

sa.d joe.

blechook, imme-

6 The Search results show where the highlighted word appears in the book. Tap one of the instances to go to that section in the book

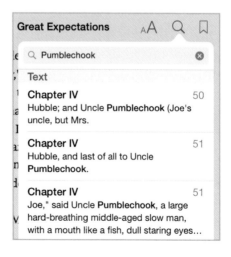

Great Expectations AА Q 🔖

Q Pumblechook ⊗

Text

Chapter IV 50
Hubble; and Uncle **Pumblechook** (Joe's uncle, but Mrs.

Chapter IV 51
Hubble, and last of all to Uncle **Pumblechook**.

Chapter IV 51
Joe," said Uncle **Pumblechook**, a large hard-breathing middle-aged slow man, with a mouth like a fish, dull staring eyes...

7 Highlight a word or phrase and tap once on the **Note** button

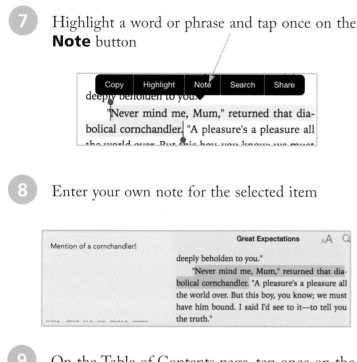

8 Enter your own note for the selected item

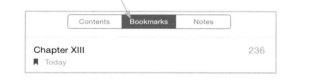

When Notes are created they are highlighted in the same way as a standard highlighted piece of text. However, there is a yellow notes icon in the margin to identify it as a note.

9 On the Table of Contents page, tap once on the **Bookmarks** button to view all of the bookmarked pages. Tap once on an item to view it

10 On the Table of Contents page, tap once on the **Notes** button to view all of

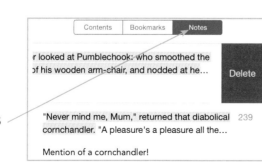

the notes you have made in the book. Swipe to the left on a note and tap once on the **Delete** button to remove it

Kindle on your iPad

The Kindle is the most popular eReader device for reading eBooks. However, it is now possible to use the Kindle app on your iPad. If you already have a Kindle account, on Amazon, then you can also import books that you have downloaded to your iPad. To use Kindle on your iPad:

Don't forget

When you first access the Kindle on your iPad you will be asked if you want to access titles that you have previously downloaded to your Kindle. After this they will appear in the Cloud section.

Hot tip

You can delete a title from the **Device** section by tapping and holding on the cover and then tapping on the **Remove from device** button. However, the title remains in the Cloud section and can be downloaded again.

Beware

If you download a book from the Kindle Cloud it only appears in the Kindle app and not in your iBooks app.

1 Download the Kindle app from the Books category in the App Store

Kindle
AMZN Mobile LLC
★★★☆☆ (16,797)

2 Tap once on this button to open the **Kindle** app

Kindle

3 If you have a Kindle account, enter the details here to register your iPad Kindle. Tap once on the **Register this Kindle** button

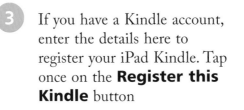

nickvandome@mac.com

••••••••

Register this Kindle

4 Tap once on this button to view the titles that are in the Kindle Cloud, i.e. have been downloaded to your Kindle account on Amazon

Cloud

5 Tap once on this button to download a title from the Kindle Cloud to your iPad

6 Tap once on the **Device** button to view items that have been downloaded to your iPad

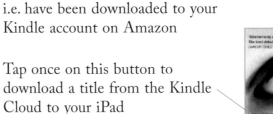

Device

9 Leisure Time

The possibilities for enjoying yourself with your iPad are huge. This chapter looks at downloading and listening to music and capturing and using photos and videos in different creative ways. It also covers some lifestyle opportunities and shows how you can obtain apps for viewing art, health, cookery and a range of games.

Buying Music

Music on the iPad can be downloaded and played using the iTunes and the Music apps respectively. iTunes links to the iTunes Store, from where music, and other content, can be bought and downloaded to your iPad. To do this:

Beware

You need to have an Apple ID with credit or debit card details added to be able to buy music from the iTunes Store.

Don't forget

If you have iTunes on another computer you can synchronize your music (and other items) that you have there to your iPad. To do this, attach the iPad to your computer (with the Dock Connector to USB Cable) and follow the setup instructions. You can check off the **Automatically Sync** options so that you can choose which items to sync. To manually update items, drag them from your iTunes Library over the iPad icon under **Devices**.

 Tap once on the **iTunes Store** app

 Tap once on the **Music** button on the iTunes toolbar at the bottom of the window

 Scroll up and down to view the featured items, or tap once on the **Genres** button to find items this way

Tap once on an item to view it. Tap once here to buy an album or tap on the button next to a song to buy that individual item

 Purchased items are included in the Music app's Library

Playing Music

Once music has been bought on iTunes it can be played on your iPad using the Music app. To do this:

 Tap once on the **Music** app

 Use these buttons to find songs by different criteria

 Tap once on a track to select it and start it playing

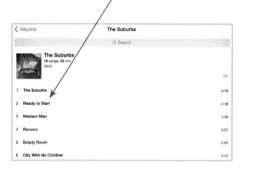

 Tap once on the middle button to pause/play a selected song

 Drag this button to increase or decrease the volume

6 Tap once on this button to repeat a song or album after it has played

7 Tap once on this button to shuffle the order of songs

Music can also be played with the iTunes Radio service (only available in the US).

To create a Playlist of songs, tap once on the **Playlist** button, then tap once on the **New** button. Give it a name and then add songs from your Library.

Music controls, including Play, Fast Forward, Rewind and Volume can also be applied in the **Control Center**, which can be accessed by swiping up from the bottom of the screen.

The camera on the back of the iPad is an iSight one and is capable of capturing high resolution photos and also high definition videos. The front-facing one is better for video calls.

Photos can also be taken by pressing the **Volume** button on the side of the iPad. This can be a good option for when it is awkward to press the virtual shutter button.

The iSight camera on the iPad Air 2 can also capture slow-motion video, with the Slo-Mo option. When a video has been captured it is also stored within the Photos app.

Taking Photos and Videos

Because of its mobility and the quality of the screen, the iPad is excellent for taking and displaying photos. Photos can be captured directly using one of the two built-in cameras (one on the front and one on the back) and then viewed, edited and shared using the Photos app. To do this:

 Tap once on the **Camera** app

 Tap once on this button to capture a photo

3 Tap once on this button to swap between the front or back cameras on the iPad

The iPad cameras can be used for different formats:

1 Swipe up or down at the side of the camera screen, underneath the shutter button, to access the different shooting options. Tap once on the **Photo** button to capture photos at full screen size

TIME-LAPSE

VIDEO

• PHOTO

SQUARE

2 Tap once on the **Square** button to capture photos at this ratio

3 Tap once on the **Time-lapse** button and press the shutter button (which appears red with ring around it) to create a time-lapse image (the camera keeps taking photos periodically until you press the shutter button again)

 Tap once on the **Video** button and press the red shutter button to take a video

Camera Settings

iCloud Sharing

Certain camera options can be applied within Settings: Several of these are to do with storing and sharing your photos via iCloud. To access these:

 Tap once on the **Settings** app

 Tap once on the **Photos & Camera** tab

3 Drag the **iCloud Photo Library** button to **On** to upload your whole photo library on your iPad to the iCloud (it remains on your iPad too). Similarly, photos on your other Apple devices can also be uploaded to the iCloud and these will be available on your iPad

iCloud Photo Library	⬤

4 Select an option for storing iCloud photos. (**Optimize iPad Storage** uses less storage as it uses device-optimized versions of your images, e.g. smaller file sizes)

Optimize iPad Storage	✓
Download and Keep Originals	

5 Drag the **Upload to My Photo Stream** button to **On** to enable all new photos and videos that you take on your iPad to be uploaded automatically to the iCloud, via Wi-Fi

Upload to My Photo Stream	⬤

6 Drag the **iCloud Photo Sharing** button to **On** to allow you to create albums within the Photos app that can then be shared with other people via iCloud

iCloud Photo Sharing	⬤

If the **iCloud Photo Library** option is **On** then your photos will all appear in the **All Photos** album in the Albums section, as well as in the Photos section. If iCloud Photo Library is **Off** there will be a **Camera Roll** album in the Albums section, where photos created on your iPad will appear.

In the Photos & Camera **Settings**, drag the **Grid** button to **On** to place a grid over the screen when you are taking photos with the Camera, if required. This can be used to help compose photos by placing subjects using the grid.

Viewing Photos

Once photos have been captured they can be viewed and organized in the Photos app. To do this:

Hot tip

Tap once on the magnifying glass icon at the top of the Years, Collections or Moments windows to search for photos according to certain criteria, such as months.

Don't forget

Tap once on the **Photos**, **Shared** and **Albums** buttons at the bottom of the **Years**, **Collections** or **Moments** windows, to view the photos in each of these sections.

1 Tap once on the **Photos** app

2 At the top level, all photos are displayed according to the years in which they were taken

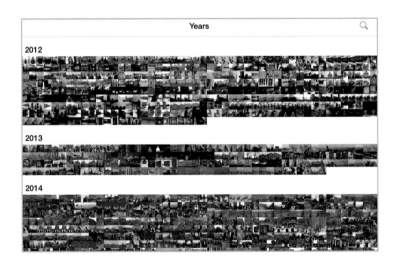

3 Tap once within the **Years** window to view photos according to specific, more defined, timescales. This is the **Collections** level. Tap once on the **Years** button to move back up one level

4 Tap once within the **Collections** window to drill down further into the photos, within the **Moments** window. Tap once on the **Collections** button to go back up one level

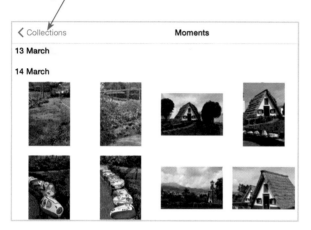

Moments are created according to the time at which the photos were added, or taken: photos added at the same time will be displayed within the same Moment.

5 Tap once on a photo within the **Moments** window to view it at full size. Tap once on the **Moments** button to go back up one level

Double-tap with one finger on an individual photo to zoom in on it. Double-tap with one finger again to zoom back out. To zoom in to a greater degree, swipe outwards with thumb and forefinger.

6 Swipe with one finger or drag here to move through all of the available photos in a specific Moment

Creating Albums

Within the Photo app it is possible to create different albums in which you can store photos. This can be a good way to organize them according to different categories and headings. To do this:

When photos are placed into albums the originals remain in the main **Photos** section.

1 Tap once on the **Albums** button

Albums

2 Tap once on this button

3 Enter a name for the new album

New Album
Enter a name for this album.

Madeira

Cancel   Save

Hot tip

Albums can be viewed as slideshows. To do this open the album and tap once on the **Slideshow** button.

Slideshow

Make the required selections and tap once on the **Start Slideshow** button.

4 Tap once on the **Save** button

5 Tap on the photos you want to include in the album

Moments   Done
Add 7 photos to "Madeira".
                            Select

6 Tap once on the **Done** button

Done

7 The new album is added to the Albums section in the Photos app

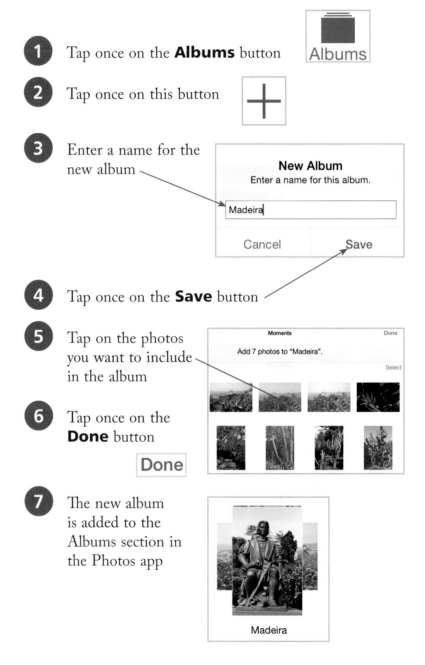

Madeira

Slideshow   Select
Slideshow Options

Transitions   Dissolve >
Play Music   ⬤
Music   None >

Start Slideshow

Selecting Photos

It is easy to take hundreds, or thousands, of digital photos and most of the time you will only want to use a selection of them. Within the Photos app it is possible to select individual photos so that you can share them, delete them or add them to albums.

Hot tip

Press and hold on a photo to access an option to copy it, rather than selecting it.

1 Access the Moments section and tap once on **Select** button

Select

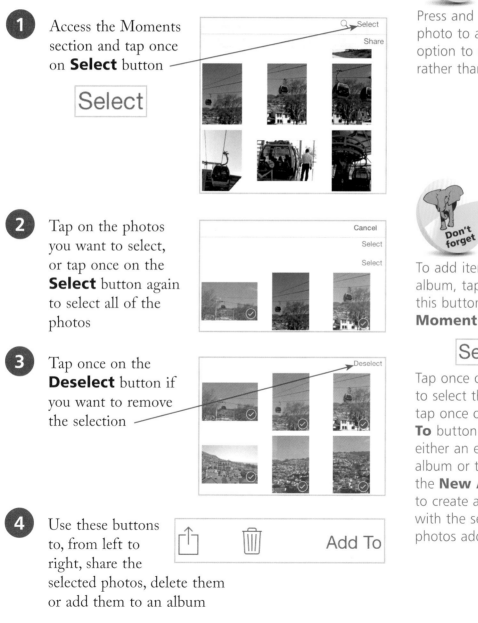

2 Tap on the photos you want to select, or tap once on the **Select** button again to select all of the photos

Don't forget

To add items to an album, tap once on this button in the **Moments** section.

Select

3 Tap once on the **Deselect** button if you want to remove the selection

Tap once on photos to select them, then tap once on the **Add To** button and select either an existing album or tap once on the **New Album** link to create a new album with the selected photos added to it.

4 Use these buttons to, from left to right, share the selected photos, delete them or add them to an album

⬆️ 🗑️ Add To

Sharing Photos

Within the Photos app there are a number of ways to share and use photos. To do this:

 Open a photo at full size and tap once on this button

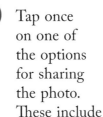 Tap once on one of the options for sharing the photo. These include messaging, emailing, sending to iCloud, adding to a contact in your Contacts app, using as your iPad wallpaper, Tweeting, sending to Facebook or Flickr, printing and copying the photo

Sharing Moments

Photo Moments can also be shared:

 Access the **Moments** section and tap once on the **Share** button

 Select **Share this moment** to share all of the photos in the moment, or **Share some photos** to make a selection

Select one of the sharing options (there may be fewer options when sharing multiple photos)

Sharing with iCloud

If you have activated the iCloud Libary and iCloud Photo Sharing (see page 143) this can be used to share your photos from the Photos app with selected people. To do this:

1 Select photos you want to share via iCloud and tap on the **Share** button

2 Tap once on the **iCloud Photo Sharing** button

3 Enter a name for the new shared photos and tap once on the **Next** button

4 Enter a recipient/recipients with whom you want to share the shared photos and tap once on the **Next** button

5 Enter a comment about your photos and tap once on the **Post** button

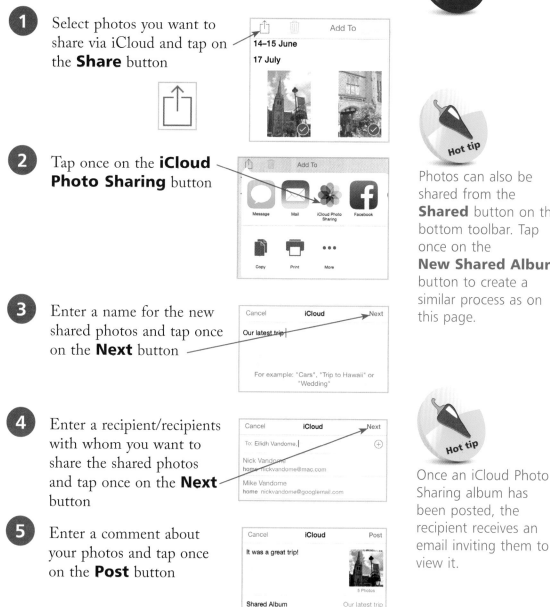

Hot tip

Photos can also be shared from the **Shared** button on the bottom toolbar. Tap once on the **New Shared Album** button to create a similar process as on this page.

Hot tip

Once an iCloud Photo Sharing album has been posted, the recipient receives an email inviting them to view it.

149

Editing Photos

The Photos app has options to perform some basic photo-editing operations. To use these:

 Open a photo at full-screen size and tap once on the **Edit** button

 The editing buttons are located on the left-hand side of the screen. Tap once on the **Auto Enhance** button to apply one-touch editing improvements

 Tap once on the **Smart Composition** button and drag the resizing handles to crop your photo. Drag the dial to the left of the photo to rotate it by degrees (to straighten it)

4 Tap once on the **Filters** button to select special effects to be applied to the photo

5 Tap once on the **Smart Adjustments** button to select color editing options. Select the option and apply the effect as required

6 For each function, tap once on the **Done** button to save the photo with the selected changes

7 Tap once on the **Cancel** button and tap once on **Discard Changes** to cancel any edits you have made

The Photo Booth app is a good one to use with grandchildren, who will enjoy experimenting with its fun and special effects. Open the app, select one of the effects and take the photo in the same way as for a standard one.

Viewing Videos

As the name suggests, the Videos app can be used to download and view video content. This is from the iTunes Store, rather than viewing your own videos. To do this:

 Tap once on the **Videos** app

 The Videos app is initially empty of content. Tap once on the **Store** button to access video content in the **iTunes Store**

Don't forget

If you rent videos from the iTunes Store you have to watch them within 30 days. Once you have started watching the video you have to finish watching it within 48 hours. Once the rental period has expired, the video is deleted from your iPad.

Tap once on the **Films** button or the **TV** button

Tap once on an item to review its content. Tap once here to download it. This is usually in the form of buying or renting a video

The downloaded video appears in the Videos app. Tap once on the cover to view its contents

  Tap once here to play a video

Photo and Video Apps

Within the App Store there is a category for Photo & Video, offering a range of apps for capturing and editing photos and videos. Some to try are:

- **iPhoto.** This is the iPad version of the popular Apple photo editing and organizing app. It is part of the iLife suite of apps and can be used as a photo library and also for a range of editing techniques, creating slideshows and sharing your photos.

- **Adobe Photoshop Express.** A mobile version of the bestselling Photoshop suite of video editing apps. Multi-Touch Gestures can be used to apply a range of editing techniques including artistic filters.

- **PowerCam HD.** A camera app that can be used to capture both photos and videos. Different special effects can be applied when the photos or videos are captured.

- **360 Panorama.** This is an app that can be used to stitch your photos together to create a 360 degree view.

- **Photo Collage HD.** An app for creating attractive collages with your photos. You can select and edit photos and add them to a collage with a range of backgrounds. It can then be shared via Facebook or Twitter.

- **iMovie.** Another app from the Apple iLife suite. This is used to edit video that you have captured. It offers functions to trim video, add transitions, captions, music and voiceovers. Once the video has been edited it can then be shared via YouTube, Facebook or iTunes.

- **Video Editor for FREE.** A video editing app that, as the name suggests, is free and a reasonable alternative to iMovie in terms of editing functionality.

- **Video Downloader.** A useful app that can be used to play most video formats through a browser interface.

- **Playable.** Another app for playing a wide range of video formats on your iPad.

Hot tip

The third app in the iLife suite is GarageBand. This is an app for creating your own music. It has a range of digital instruments that can be used to record tracks and also pre-recorded loops that can be added.

Hot tip

If you cannot find a certain app under the **iPad Only** heading in the App Store, tap once on the button and select the **iPhone Only** option. These can be downloaded for the iPad too, although they will have a smaller screen area to view the app.

Hot tip

Most top museums have some form of app available. If there is not one for a museum in which you are interested try contacting the museum and asking if they are planning on developing an app.

Discovering Art

It is always a pleasure to view works of art in real life, but the next best alternative is to be able to look at them on the high-resolution Retina display on your iPad. As far as viewing art goes, there are two options:

- Apps that contain general information about museums and art galleries.

- Apps that display the works belonging to museums and art galleries.

In general, type the name of a museum or art gallery into the App Store Search box to see if there is an applicable app. Some apps to look at are:

- **Guggenheim Bilbao.** Information and examples from the iconic museum in Bilbao.

- **Museums and Galleries of London.** A general guide to 30 museums and galleries in London. With reviews and photos and also opening times and prices.

- **New York Museum Guide.** This is a comprehensive guide including opening hours, bookings and maps.

- **Musée du Louvre HD.** High-resolution images and descriptions of the world-famous art of the Louvre.

- **Museums Locator.** A general museum app for locating establishments around the world.

- **50 painting masterpieces you must see in Madrid.** A detailed guide to the Prado Museum in Madrid, including descriptions of 50 famous paintings.

- **Uffizi Touch.** Although this is more expensive than the other apps above, this offers a sumptuous tour of the works in the Uffizi Gallery in Florence.

Creating Pictures

If you want to branch out from just looking at works of art, you can try creating some of your own too. There is a range of drawing and painting apps that can be used to let your creative side run riot. Most of these function in a similar fashion in terms of creating pictures:

 Drawing tools appear at the bottom of the app

 Swipe from left to right to access different tool options and selections

3 Tap and draw with your finger on the screen to create a picture

Some apps to try are:

- **Brushes.** One of the most powerful painting apps with a wide range of tools and features, including up to six layers in each painting and five blend modes.

- **Drawing Pad.** Similar to Brushes, but not at such a high level. Suitable as a first option for iPad painting.

- **Inspire Pro.** A wide range of blending features makes this one of the best painting apps around.

- **Learn to Draw Digital Sketchbook.** A drawing app that has tutorials for learning how to draw and also examples that can be used as templates and copied over.

- **SketchBook Express.** A sketching app at a similar level to Brushes for painting.

Hot tip

You may find using a touch screen stylus makes drawing easier.

Don't forget

Most drawing and painting apps have an **Undo** function and also an eraser that can be used to remove unwanted items.

Hot tip

If you are using your iPad in the kitchen, keep it away from direct contact with cooking areas, to avoid splashes. If there is a risk of this, cover the iPad with cling-film/plastic wrap to give it some protection.

Don't forget

Many recipe apps have a facility for uploading your own recipes, so that they can be shared with other people.

Cooking with your iPad

Your iPad may not be quite clever enough to cook dinner for you, but there are enough cookery apps to ensure that you will never go without a good meal with your iPad at your side. Some to look at are:

- **AllRecipes Video Cookbook.** Instead of just reading recipes, use this app to watch them being made in step-by-step videos.

- **BigOven 250,000+ Recipes.** As the name suggests, thousands of recipes to keep you busy in the kitchen for as long as you want. You can also store your grocery lists here.

- **Cake Recipes.** To get your mouth watering, this app has hundreds of cake ideas, from the simple to the exotic.

- **Green Kitchen.** A must for vegetarians, with stylish and creative recipes for organic and vegetarian food.

- **Jamie's Recipes.** An app featuring the recipes of the well-known chef Jamie Oliver. (Most well-known chefs now have their own cooking apps: just enter the name of a chef in the App Store to see the options).

- **Recipes Starter Kit.** For the less experienced chefs, this is a good way to gain confidence in the kitchen.

- **Slow Cooker Recipes.** Put your dish together with this app, leave it in the slow cooker and then enjoy it several hours later when ready.

- **Sweet Baking.** As well as covering cakes and cookies this app also has recipes for a variety of breads.

Staying Healthy

Most people are health conscious these days and the App Store has a category covering Health & Fitness. This includes apps about general fitness, healthy eating, relaxation and yoga. Some to try are:

- **Calorie Counter and Diet Tracker.** If you want to stick to a diet this app can help you along the way. You need to register, which is free, and then you can set your own diet plan and fitness profile.

- **Daily Workouts.** Some of the exercise apps are for dedicated gym-goers. If you are looking for something a bit less extreme this app could fit the bill. A range of exercises that will keep you fit without the need to be a body builder.

- **Daily Yoga.** Audio and video instructions for timed sessions and over 30 yoga poses.

- **Menu Planner.** A dieting aid that enables you to create your own menu plans.

- **MyPilatesGuru.** Use this app to work through over 80 pilates exercise sessions. You can also create your own sessions and save them to repeat.

- **Serenity.** Over 30 videos and sound files to help you relax or fall asleep.

- **Sleep Pillow Sounds.** Everyone enjoys a good night's sleep and this app can help you achieve it. A collection of ambient sounds are played to help you relax and sleep.

- **Universal Breathing.** Designed to promote slow breathing, to help with a range of health conditions including high blood pressure, migraines and asthma.

There is also a **Medical** category in the App Store that contains a range of apps covering medical topics and subjects.

The version of iOS 8 for the iPhone also has a built-in Health app. However, this is not provided with the iPad, partly as it is designed to work with the iPhone and the Apple Watch, due to be released in 2015.

If you have a genuine medical complaint, get it checked out by your doctor, rather than trying to find a solution through an app or on the Web.

Playing Games

Although computer games may seem like the preserve of the younger generation this is definitely not the case. Not all computer games are of the shoot-em-up or racing variety and the App Store also contains puzzles and versions of popular board games. There are two ways to access games:

- Via the App Store under the Games category.

- Via the Game Center built-in iPad app. This is usually used if you want to compare scores with other users or if you want to play games simultaneously with other people online in a multi-player game.

Some games to try are:

- **Chess.** Pit your wits against this chess app. Various settings can be applied for each game, such as the level of difficulty.

- **Checkers.** Similar to the Chess app, but for Checkers (Draughts). Hints are also available to help develop your skills and knowledge.

- **Mahjong.** A version of the popular Chinese game, but this is a matching game for single players, rather than playing with other people.

- **Scrabble.** An iPad version of the best-selling word game that can be played with up to four people.

- **Solitaire.** An old favorite, the card game where you have to build sequences and remove all of the cards.

- **Sudoku.** The numbers game where you have to fill different grids with numbers 1-9, without having any of the same in a row or column.

- **Tetris.** One of the original computer games, where you have to piece together falling shapes to make lines.

- **Words With Friends.** Similar to Scrabble, an online word game, played with other users.

Don't forget

As well as the games here, there is also a full range of other types of games in the App Store.

10 Getting on the Map

With an iPad and the Maps app the world is your oyster. This chapter shows how to find locations and directions.

Beware

To ensure that the Maps app works most effectively, it has to be enabled for Location Services so that it can use your current location (**Settings > Privacy > Location Services > Maps** and select **While Using the App** under **Allow Location Access**).

160

Hot tip

Tap on the icon in Step 2 to change it into the active compass, below. With this activated, when you change position, the map moves with you at the same time.

Looking Around Maps

With the Maps app you need never again wonder about where a location is, or worry about getting directions to somewhere. As long as you are connected to Wi-Fi or have a 3G/4G network, you will be able to do the following:

- Search maps around the world
- Find addresses, famous buildings or landmarks
- Get directions between different locations
- View traffic conditions

Viewing maps

To view your current location and maps around the world:

1 Tap once on the **Maps** app

2 Tap once on this button to view your current location

3 Double-tap with one finger on a map to zoom in (or swipe outwards with thumb and forefinger)

4 Tap once with two fingers on a map to zoom out (or pinch inwards with thumb and forefinger)

Types of Maps

The standard view that is used in Maps can be changed so that you can view maps according to satellite and hybrid views. To do this:

 Tap here to access the map options

 Maps can be viewed as **Standard**, **Hybrid** and **Satellite**. Tap on one of the options here to view a particular style of map

Don't forget

Hybrid and Satellite maps can be zoomed in and out on, in the same way as for the Standard map view.

Hot tip

Tap once on the **Show Traffic** button to show any traffic congestion on the map being viewed. Red markings indicate an average speed below 25mph; yellow, 25-50mph; and green, over 50mph.

Finding Locations

Within Maps you can search for addresses, locations, landmarks, intersections or businesses. To do this:

1 Enter an item into the Search box

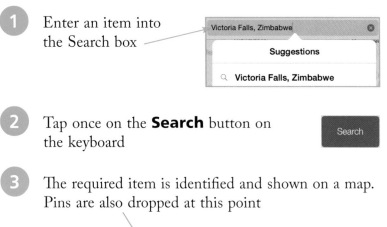

2 Tap once on the **Search** button on the keyboard

3 The required item is identified and shown on a map. Pins are also dropped at this point

You can also search for locations by postcodes or zip codes.

4 Locations can be viewed from a local, national or international level

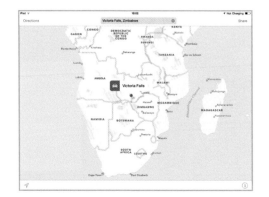

Using Pins

Pins are used to identify locations and also display additional information about locations or addresses. They can also be used to access photos for a location.

In addition to pins that are dropped when you find a location, you can also drop your own pins at any point. To use pins:

1. Tap once on a pin to view its options

2. Tap once on this button to access additional information about the selected item

3. Tap once on the buttons under **Location** to add an item to your Contacts, or add to your Safari bookmarks, or share it via email, iMessage, Facebook or Twitter using the **Share** button

4. To drop your own pin, tap and hold on a location. This drops a purple pin as opposed to the red ones. Tap and hold on a pin and drag it around to change its position

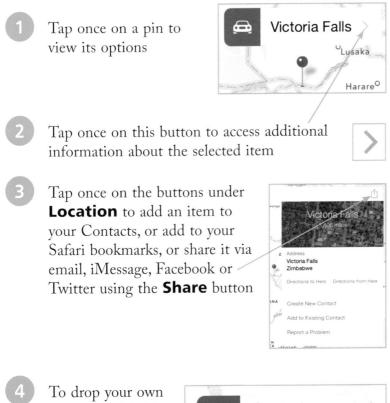

Tap on the **Directions** button on the pin options bar to find directions to the selected location.

Getting Directions

Finding your way around is an important element of using maps and this can be done with the Directions function:

1 Tap once on the **Directions** button

> Directions

2 By default, your current location is used for the **Start** field. If you want to change this, tap once and enter a new location or address

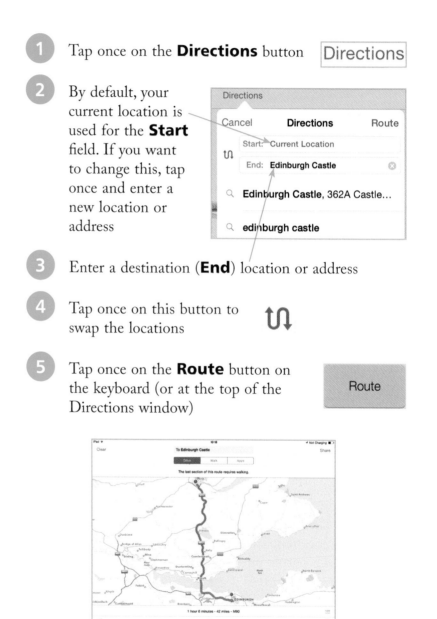

Beware

If you enter the name of a landmark you may also be shown other items that have the same name, such as businesses.

3 Enter a destination (**End**) location or address

4 Tap once on this button to swap the locations

5 Tap once on the **Route** button on the keyboard (or at the top of the Directions window)

> Route

6 The route is shown on the map

7 Tap once on the **Start** button in the middle-bottom of the screen to get directions

8 The route is shown on the map with directions for each section

Hot tip

Depending on the directions, the map will be zoomed in and out as you access each instruction.

9 Swipe to the left and right here to view the next, or previous, set of directions for the route

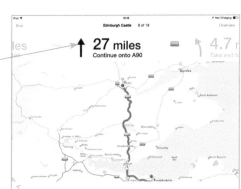

Don't forget

To get back to the Start view, tap once on the **End** button.

10 Tap once on this button in the bottom right-hand corner of the screen to view details of the route for the selected mode of transport. The default option is by car

11 At the top of the Route window

To **Edinburgh Castle**

| Drive | Walk | Apps |

(before you tap the **Start** button) tap once on these buttons to view options for walking and also accessing apps for public transport

Using Flyover Tour

One of the innovative features in the Maps app in iOS 8 is the Flyover Tour function. This is an animated Flyover Tour of certain location that gives you a 3D tour of a city in Satellite view. To view a Flyover Tour:

166

1 If the Flyover Tour function is available for the location you are viewing there will be a

3D Flyover Tour option. Tap on this once to start the Flyover Tour (from any map view)

2 The tour starts and takes you through an aerial 3D tour of the main sights of the location

3 The tour will end automatically, or you can tap once on the **End Flyover Tour** button at any time

End Flyover Tour

11 Traveling Companion

This chapter shows why you should never be without your iPad when you are traveling or on vacation.

Traveling with your iPad

When you go traveling, there are a few essentials that you have to consider: passport, money and insurance to name three. To this you can add your iPad: it is a perfect traveling companion that can help you plan your trip and keep you informed and entertained when you are away from home.

Uses for traveling

There are a lot of App Store apps that can be used for different aspects of traveling. However, the built-in apps can also be put to good use before and during your travels:

Hot tip

The Clock app can also be used so that you can keep an eye on the time in different parts of the world.

- **Maps.** Use this app for accessing maps of your destinations, finding directions and viewing images of areas to which you are traveling.

- **Notes.** Create lists of items to pack or landmarks that you want to visit.

- **Contacts.** Keep your Contacts app up-to-date so that you can use it to send postcards to friends and family. You can also use it to access phone numbers if you want to phone home.

- **Reminders.** Set reminders for important tasks, such as changing foreign currency, buying tickets and details of flights.

Beware

You can also use the Videos app to download movies and TV shows from the iTunes Store. However, these will take up a significant amount of space on your iPad in terms of storage.

- **Music.** Use this app to play your favorite music while you are traveling, or relaxing at your destination.

- **Photos.** Store photos of your trip with this app and play them back as a slideshow when you get back home.

- **FaceTime.** If you have a Wi-Fi connection at your destination you will be able to keep in touch with video calls (as long as the recipient has FaceTime too).

- **iBooks.** Instead of dragging lots of heavy books around, use this app for your vacation library.

Planning your Trip

A lot of the fun of going on vacation and traveling is in the planning. The anticipation of researching new places to visit and explore can whet the appetite for what is ahead. The good news is that you can plan your whole itinerary while sitting in an armchair with your iPad on your lap. In the App Store there are apps for organizing your itinerary and others for exploring the possibilities of where you can go:

Tripit

This is an app for keeping all of your travel details in one place. You have to register, which is free, and you can then enter your own itinerary details. Whenever you receive an email confirmation for a flight, hotel or car hire that you have booked, you can email this to your Tripit account (**plans@tripit.com**) and this will be added to your itinerary.

GetPacked

A great way to get peace of mind before you leave. This app generates a packing list and to-do lists to check before you leave, based on questions that you answer about your vacation and travel arrangements. You can then select items to include on your packing list, from clothes to documents and medical items.

Although there is a small fee for the GetPacked app, it is well worth it as it covers everything you will need to consider before you leave.

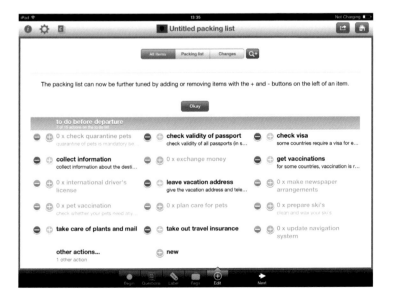

...cont'd

Cool Escapes Hotels & Resorts

Guaranteed to give you itchy feet, this app matches quality hotels with some amazing locations around the world.
You can explore by map, country, area, hotel type and price, to find the perfect combination.

Beware

Some maps apps are free to download but there is then a fee to buy the associated maps.

World Travel Atlas

A comprehensive travel companion that offers a world atlas that contains information about countries, cities, landmarks, airports and events. Navigate around the atlas with the same swiping and tapping gestures as with the Maps app. Tap once on an item to access a wealth of information about it.

Viewing Flights

Flying is a common part of modern life and although you do not have to book separate flights for a vacation (if it is part of a package) there are a number of apps for booking flights and also following the progress of those in the air:

Skyscanner

This app can be used to find flights at airports around the world. Enter your details such as leaving airport, destination and dates of travel. The results show a range of available options, covering different price ranges.

FlightRadar24

If you like viewing the path of flights that are in the air, or need to check if flights are going to be delayed, this app provides this inflight information. Flights are shown according to flight number and airline.

Flight apps need to have an Internet connection in order to show real-time flight information.

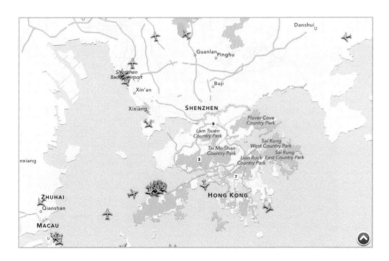

AirportZoom

As well as showing real-time flight details, this app also has airline departure and arrival information and maps of airport terminals and flight gates.

FlightAware Flight Tracker

Another app for tracking flights, showing arrivals and departures and also information about delays.

Finding Hotels

The Internet is a perfect vehicle for finding good value hotel rooms around the world. When hotels have spare capacity, this can quickly be relayed to associated websites, where users can usually benefit from cheap prices and special offers. There are plenty of apps that have details of thousands of hotels around the world, such as:

TripAdvisor
One of the top travel apps, this not only has hotel information but also restaurants, activities and flights. Enter a destination in the search box and then navigate through the available options.

Hotels.com
A stylish app that enables you to enter search keywords or tap once on a hotel on the Home screen to view options for this location.

Booking.com
Another good, fully-featured hotel app that provides a comprehensive service and excellent prices.

LateRooms.com
An app that specializes in getting the best prices by dealing with rooms that are available at short notice. Some genuine bargains can be found here, for hotels of all categories.

Hot tip

Most hotel apps have reviews of all of the listed establishments. It is always worth reading these as it gives you a view from the people who have actually been there.

Converting Currency

Money is always important in life and never more so than when you are on vacation and possibly following a budget. It is therefore imperative to know the exchange rate of currencies in different countries compared to your own. Two apps that provide this service are:

XE Currency

This app delivers information about exchange rates for all major world currencies and also a wealth of background information such as high and low rates and historical charts.

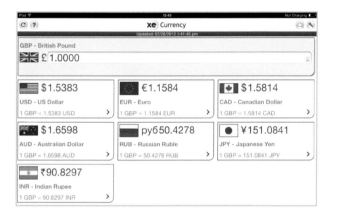

Hot tip

When changing currency, either at home or abroad, always shop around to get the best rate. Using credit cards abroad usually attracts a supplementary charge too.

Currency

This app provides up-to-date exchange rates for over 150 currencies and 100 countries.

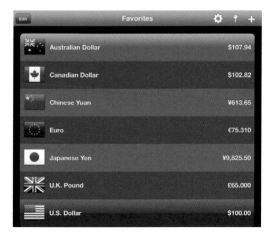

Travel Apps

Everyone has different priorities and preferences when they are on vacation. The following are some apps from the App Store that cover a range of activities and services:

- **1000 Places To See Before You Die.** A collection of stunning and unforgettable destinations and locations around the world. Impressive photography makes it all the more appealing and you can also browse maps.

- **Disneyland Paris.** If you are entertaining your grandchildren at Disneyland Paris, this app will help you survive the experience. Maps, show times and descriptions of features help you organize all aspects of your visit.

- **Fotopedia Heritage.** A selection of stunning photography of World Heritage sites. Guaranteed to make you want to head for the airport.

- **Florida Theme Parks.** Another one for the family and grandchildren. Everything you need to know about these popular tourist attractions.

- **Google Earth.** Not just a travel aid, this app enables you to search around the globe and look at photos and 3D maps of your favorite places.

Don't forget

Fotopedia has other photography apps, covering areas including National Parks, Wild Friends and Women of the World.

- **Hailo.** For anyone visiting London, New York, Dublin, Toronto and other large cities (more being added), this app allows you to hail a cab, at the tap of a button.

- **Kayak.** A useful all-round app that compares hundreds of travel websites to get the best prices for flights, hotels and car rental. You can also create your own itineraries.

- **Language apps.** If you want to learn a new language for your travels, there is a wide range of apps for this. These are located in either the Travel or Education categories in the App Store.

- **Laplication.** For something a little bit off the beaten track, use this app to see the wonders of Lapland, including the incredible Northern Lights.

- **myLanguage Free Translator.** If you do not have the time, or inclination, to learn a new language, try this app to translate 59 different languages.

- **National Geographic Traveler.** Subscribe to this app to get an endless supply of high-quality travel features, photography and travel ideas.

- **New York Subway Map.** Use this app to help get around the Big Apple via the Subway. Plan your journeys and view live updates about stations and routes.

There are apps for displaying train times and details, but these are usually specific to your geographical location rather than covering a range of different countries.

175

...cont'd

- **Over 40 Magnifier and Flashlight.** Not just for traveling, this fantastic app acts as a torch and a magnifying glass all in one.

- **P&O Cruises.** Find some of your favorite cruises with this app that displays the full brochure of P&O Cruises.

- **Paris Transport Map.** One free map for travel options around one of the great cities in the world.

- **Photo Translator.** Ever wondered what signs in a foreign language mean? This app can translate them for you: take a photo with your iPad and the app gives you a translation of the sign, or phrase.

- **Phrasebook.** Keep up with what the locals are saying in different countries with this app that has useful phrases in 25 languages.

- **Sixt Rent a Car.** Use this app for car rental in 90 countries around the world.

- **London Tube Map.** Find your way around London with this digital version of the iconic Tube Map. It includes live departure boards and station information.

- **Urbanspoon.** Another app for finding restaurants on your vacation. Enter your location, shake your iPad and the app uses a slot machine interface to come up with suggestions. Covers USA, Canada, UK, Australia and New Zealand.

- **Weather+.** An app for showing the weather in locations around the world, including hourly updates.

- **Wi-Fi Finder.** It is always useful to be able to access Wi-Fi when you are on vacation, and sometimes essential. This app locates Wi-Fi hotspots in 650,000 locations in 144 countries worldwide.

- **Yelp.** Covering a range of services, this app locates restaurants, shops, services and places of interest in cities around the world.

Beware

The Phrasebook app comes with one free language. After that you have to pay a small fee for each language that you want to use.

12 Practical Matters

This chapter looks at security on the iPad and locating a lost device. It also shows how to use it for financial matters.

Setting Restrictions

Within the iPad Settings app there are options for restricting types of content that can be viewed and also actions that can be performed. These include:

- Turning off certain apps so that they cannot be used

- Enabling changes to certain functions

- Restricting content that is viewed using specific apps

When setting restrictions, they can be locked so that no-one else can change them. To set and lock restrictions:

Hot tip

It is a good idea to set up some restrictions on your iPad if young children and grandchildren are going to have access to it.

1. Tap once on the **Settings** app

2. Tap once on the **General** tab

3. Tap once on the **Restrictions** link

Restrictions	Off >

4. The restrictions are grayed-out, i.e. they have not been enabled for use yet

‹ General	**Restrictions**

Enable Restrictions

ALLOW:

	Safari	
	Camera	
	FaceTime	
	iTunes	

5. Tap once on the **Enable Restrictions** link

Enable Restrictions

Type on the keypad to set a passcode for enabling and disabling restrictions

 Re-enter the passcode

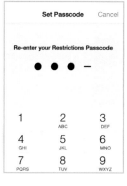

8 All of the Restrictions options become available. Drag these buttons **On** or **Off** to disable certain apps. If this is done they will no longer be visible on the Home screen. Tap once on the links under **Allowed Content** to specify restrictions for certain types of content, such as music, movies, books and apps

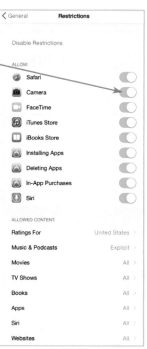

Beware

If you forget the passcode for unlocking your iPad it will become disabled for a period of time after you have entered the wrong passcode a number of times. Eventually, it will lock completely. It can be reset by using a computer with which the iPad was last synced and there are details about this on the Apple website Support pages. However, to avoid this, ensure that you have a note of the iPad's passcode, but keep it away from the iPad.

179

Finding your iPad

No-one likes to think the worst, but if your iPad is lost or stolen, help is at hand. The Find My iPad function (operated through the iCloud service) allows you to send a message and an alert to a lost iPad and also remotely lock it or even wipe its contents. This gives added peace of mind, knowing that even if your iPad is lost or stolen its contents will not necessarily be compromised. To set up Find My iPad:

1 Tap once on the **Settings** app

2 Tap once on the **iCloud** tab

3 Tap once on the **Find My iPad** link and drag the button to **On** to be able to find your iPad on a map

Location Services must be turned On to enable the Find My iPad service (**Settings > Privacy** and turn **Location Services** On).

4 Tap once on the **Allow** button to enable the Find My iPad functionality

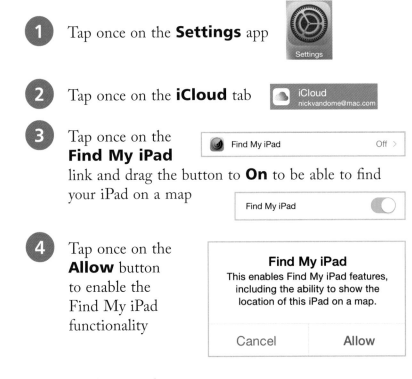

Find My iPad   Off >

Find My iPad

Find My iPad
This enables Find My iPad features, including the ability to show the location of this iPad on a map.

Cancel   Allow

Finding a lost iPad
Once you have set up Find My iPad you can search for it through the iCloud service. To do this:

1 Log in to your iCloud account at **www.icloud.com**

2 Tap once on the **Find My iPhone** button (this also works for the iPad)

3 Tap once on the **All Devices** button and select your iPad. It is identified and its current location is displayed on the map

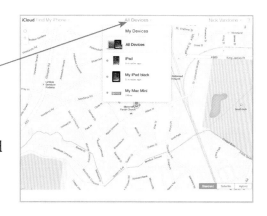

4 Tap once on the green circle to view details about when your iPad was located

Don't forget

Click once on the **Erase iPad** button to delete the iPad's contents.

181

5 Tap once here to send a sound alert to your iPad

6 Tap once here to lock your iPad

7 Enter a passcode so that no-one else can access the contents on your iPad

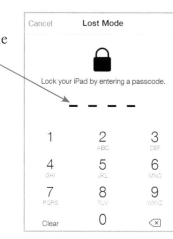

Hot tip

If you are using Family Sharing (see pages 40-45) you can use Find My iPhone to locate the devices of other Family Sharing members. This can be done from your online iCloud account, or by downloading the Find My iPhone app from the App Store.

Locking your iPad

As shown in Chapter Two, the screen can be auto-locked, but this does not have a security control. If you want to make sure that no-one else can access your iPad's content a passcode can be set for unlocking the screen. To do this:

On the iPad Air 2 and iPad Mini 3, the option in Step 2 is for Touch ID and Passcode. This can be used to create a fingerprint Touch ID for unlocking your iPad with the Home button and your own unique fingerprint.

1 Tap once on the **Settings** app

2 Tap once on the **Passcode** tab

🔒 Passcode

3 Tap once on the **Turn Passcode On** link

Turn Passcode On

4 Enter a passcode and tap once on the **Next** button

Cancel   **Set Passcode**   Next

Enter a passcode

●●●●|

5 Re-enter the passcode and tap once on the **Done** button

Cancel   **Set Passcode**   Done

Re-enter your passcode

●●●●

Once the passcode has been set, tap once on the **Require Passcode** button to specify when the passcode is activated. This can be immediately, or over a period of time.

6 The passcode has to be entered to access the iPad for use every time it has been locked

Enter Passcode
○ ○ ○ ○

1 2 ABC 3 DEF
4 GHI 5 JKL 6 MNO
7 PQRS 8 TUV 9 WXYZ
0 Cancel

Avoiding Viruses

As far as security from viruses on the iPad is concerned there is good news and bad news:

- The good news is that, due to its architecture, most apps on the iPad do not communicate with each other so, even if there was a virus, it is unlikely that it would infect the whole iPad. Also, there are relatively few viruses being aimed at the iPad, particularly compared to those for Windows PCs.

- The bad news is that no computer system is immune from viruses and malware, and complacency is one of the biggest enemies of computer security. There have been some instances of photos in iCloud being accessed and hacked, but this was more to do with password security, or lack of, rather than viruses.

iPad security

Apple takes security on the iPad very seriously and one way that this manifests itself is in the fact it is designed so that different apps do not talk to each other. This means that if there was a virus in an app then it would be hard for it to transfer to others and therefore spread across the iPad. Apple's own apps are the exception to this, but as they are developed and checked by Apple there is very little chance of them being infected by viruses.

Antivirus options

There are a few apps in the App Store that deal with antivirus issues, although not actually removing viruses:

- **VirusBarrier.** This checks files that are copied onto your iPad, via email or online services, to ensure that they are virus-free.

- **McAfee** apps. The online security firm has a number of apps which cover issues such as privacy of data and security of passwords.

- **Norton Snap QR Code Reader**. This reads code from websites to check for viruses and malware.

Malware is short for malicious software, designed to harm your computer or access and distribute information from it.

Apple also checks apps that are provided through the App Store and this process is very robust. This does not mean that it is impossible for a virus to infect the iPad so keep an eye on the Apple website to see if there are any details about iPad viruses.

Dealing with Money

We all like to keep track of our money and, although it may not be as much fun as reading books or looking at photos, it is a necessary task that can be undertaken on the iPad.

Some general financial apps are looked at on page 186, but one of the most common uses for financial matters is online banking. This is where you can use banking apps to access your bank accounts.

Banking apps are specific to your geographical location, i.e. the banks that operate in your country. Most banking apps operate in a similar way:

Beware

If you are logging into your online banking service, make sure any Remember Me log in details functions are checked off, particularly if other people have access to your iPad.

 1 You have to first register for the online service. Once you have done this, tap on the Log On button to access your account details

Don't forget

Online banking sites can also be accessed through the Web using Safari.

 2 General information is also available through the app, such as branch locations and contact details

Looking at Property

If you are looking to move home, or buy property as an investment, your iPad is a great starting point. There are a lot of real estate apps that provide high quality color photos of all parts of properties for sale.

As with banking apps, real estate apps are specific to your geographical location and they all have a search facility for looking for properties in different areas. The search results can usually be filtered by criteria such as price, number of bedrooms and property type. To use a real estate app:

 Browse properties according to area

Some property apps also allow you to book appointments to view properties in person.

 Tap once on a property to view more details. This usually includes photos of all of the rooms and a full description of the property

Financial Apps

Within the Finance category of the App Store there are apps for managing your personal finances, viewing share prices and organizing your bank accounts and bills. Some to look at are:

- **Account Tracker.** A useful app for keeping track of your expenditure. It can be used to monitor multiple bank accounts and also set alerts and reminders for paying bills.

- **Calculator.** For working out your own finances, this calculator provides a large, attractive interface with plenty of functionality.

- **Bloomberg.** This is an app for following stocks and shares. You can add any shares that you own and view live prices while markets are open (with a 15 minute delay). There is also a financial news service.

- **HomeBudget.** An app for managing your household incomes and expenses. It also supports charts and graphs so you can compare expenditure over periods of time.

- **Meter Readings.** Useful for keeping an eye on your fuel consumption, this app helps you to save money by monitoring your utility readings. Enter the readings and your usage and costs are displayed in user-friendly graphs to show where savings can be made.

- **Mint Personal Finance.** Another general finance app for managing your money and monitoring budgets.

- **Money for iPad Free.** As well as being used to manage bills and view all of your accounts, this app also provides useful planning features and reminders.

- **Pocket Expense.** Another in the range of apps with which you can monitor bank accounts, track bills, view transactions and see where you can save money.

- **SharePrice.** Another app for seeing how your share portfolio is doing. Real-time share information, market news and profit/loss details are provided.

Hot tip

With your iPad and an Internet connection, you should always be able to keep an eye on your shares portfolio as well as buying and selling shares, wherever you are.